"I find this book helpful to me personally because I was diagnosed with bipolar type 1 four years ago. That diagnosis changed my life drastically and the truth did hurt me. I was ill. But I got the help I needed and was able to get back on my feet with the support of family, friends, and my psychiatrist. I wish I had this book when I was first diagnosed. This book is useful, and I recommend it to anyone who knows someone with bipolar 1."
— **Karen Nguyen.**

"I have never met the author personally, but I feel as if I have known her a long time such is the engaging and conversational way she writes. The overarching impression from reading this book is this lady knows what she is talking about having personally experienced the ongoing nightmare of bipolar. She has lived and experienced every chapter in the book herself. This is NOT some dry academic book stitched together by someone that hasn't been there, done that. There is something here for everyone no matter what stage of the journey you are at through this illness. You will laugh at some of the exploits the author has been involved in, you will cry at the depths to which the human mind can sink, but most of all you will come away with a feeling of hope that there is light at the end of the tunnel of bipolar. Recommended."
— **Grahame Cossum**, author of three books on Depression.

"Sally Alter's book is a heartfelt and experiential description of bipolar disorder. I believe it will be extremely helpful to those struggling with this terrible illness, or friends and family members who need to understand what it is like to suffer with bipolar 1. I feel this book would also be helpful to those interested in psychology and researching bipolar disorder."
— **Jon Shore**, Psychotherapist,
(specializing in depression and anxiety disorders).

"An incredibly honest, insightful look at the ways in which bipolar disorder affects every area of your life. Sally gives a fantastic blend of medical advice and personal experience that feels as though she is right there beside you, hopeful and encouraging, shining light towards the end of the tunnel. It will keep you reading all night!"
— **Michele Abbott**, B.Sc. Quora writer.

BIPOLAR 1
RESCUE PLAN

A practical guide for
you and your family

From the Author of *How to Live with Bipolar*

Sally Alter http://sallyalter.com

Cover design & formatting: Rew Mitchell, rewkachu.com

To Hal Robinson, Kathy Pennell, Pamala Osborne, Patrick Nolan and Marion Harris with thanks for their unwavering support while writing this book.

Famous people
with bipolar disorder

Kanye West
Mariah Carey
Carrie Fisher
Mel Gibson
Demi Lovato
Maria Bamford
Catherine Zeta-Jones
Frank Sinatra
David LaChapelle
Sinead O'Connor
Jean-Claude Van Damme
Jane Pauley
Patty Duke
Linda Hamilton
Mariette Hartley
Selena Gomez
Scott Stapp
Maurice Benard
David Harbour

Amy Winehouse
Halsey
Richard Dreyfuss
Russell Brand
Kurt Cobain
Grahame Greene
Nina Simone
Sir. Winston Churchill
Vincent Van Gogh
Virginia Wolf
Ernest Hemingway
Buzz Aldrin
Florence Nightingale
Sting
Isaac Newton
William Blake
Beethoven
Theodore Roosevelt

PART THREE
COMPLICATIONS OF BIPOLAR 1

PART SIX
MANAGEMENT OF BIPOLAR 1

Introduction

If you are finding it difficult to manage your bipolar 1 disorder, then this is the book for you. It is brimming with practical advice and tips and tricks to help you better manage your life.

Perhaps you have just been diagnosed and don't know where to start. Or maybe you've had bipolar 1 for a long time and tried everything but failed. You may even have had problems at home, at work, or with making friends. Whatever your situation, if you are still suffering with the symptoms of this debilitating illness, I will be able to help you.

It is very disheartening when you are trying as hard as you can, but no matter what you do things keep going wrong. That's when you are inclined to blame yourself which makes you feel even worse.

I know exactly how you feel because I have had a lifetime of bipolar 1 and have had many ups and downs, as well. Now, I am happy to say that I have been totally free of symptoms for three years and am excited to share the key to my success with you.

You will find this book covers all kinds of topics, maybe things you hadn't even thought of before. You may like to try new recipes that can help you eat a nutritious diet, learn how to do creative visualization, and try new organizational skills to keep you on track.

I have it all here for you in this book. As you will see, I have written it to help you get well and stay well.

This book will cover the basics of the diagnosis, talk about the incidence, the causes, similar illnesses, and the effects on the family as well as what it is like to live with bipolar 1.

We will also talk about all the symptoms of the disorder, including mania, depression, psychosis, mixed features, and rapid cycling. And, because anxiety and panic attacks are so common with a bipolar diagnosis, we will talk about this as well.

We shall discuss what it is like to feel overwhelmed, face bipolar aging, menopause, and substance abuse. And I will also talk about all the blips you experience between episodes.

The book will also cover topics like psychiatrists, medications, psychotherapists, and different forms of therapy as these are the first line of call in your treatment plan. I have also listed some recipes you might like to try on the Mediterranean diet. We will discuss yoga, tai chi, qigong, meditation, mindfulness, and you will even find creative exercises you can practice with a friend.

I will also talk about the things you can do to manage bipolar 1 properly like routines, triggers, coping skills, relationships, mood charts, and support systems.

Unlike other books on bipolar disorder which only tell you about things you already know, I have included many practical things you can do to get well and stay well.

Don't worry. You don't have to be at the mercy of your symptoms. You have a say in your illness, and I will show you what to do. You may have failed before, and you may fail along the way, but there is hope in this book for a better life with bipolar 1 disorder.

Let's get started.

Family and friends

For the family

First, let me thank you for reading this book. You may read it with your loved one or on your own, but I am glad you are here to learn all you can about bipolar 1 disorder.

You may have just learned that your family member has bipolar 1, and it can be a total shock. How could this happen to him or to her? They were such a good student and a happy child it is hard to imagine that they are now faced with this terrible illness. What will become of them? Will they be able to hold down a career? Will they be able to marry, have children? All these questions will be swirling round in your head, and you will want answers.

You may experience several different emotions. You may feel angry, sad, or even guilty that you are somehow to blame for what has happened to your loved one. This is perfectly natural. It is hard to come to terms with a diagnosis like this.

It is quite true that bipolar disorder does run in families. In fact, a child of a bipolar parent has a 25% chance of inheriting the disease themselves. You may start to look for other signs of it in your family and suddenly see your relatives in a different light. You may also worry about the stigma, and what to tell others. There is undoubtedly a stigma attached to this illness, even in the 21st Century. The reason for this problem is one of ignorance. When people are educated about the disease, they don't need to be afraid of it. It is not contagious.

Your loved one may have been ill for quite some time with no improvement in their condition. You may have seen them in depression and mania, even psychosis, and wondered what to do. You might think that they haven't tried enough to get well when this is never the case with bipolar disorder. It is nothing to do with personality or character at all. Not even willpower. But I do understand, it is very difficult to watch your loved one suffer, and it is not always easy to know what to do for the best. I hope this book will show you the way, so that your loved one can feel supported as this is what they need.

Whichever way you look at it, a diagnosis of bipolar 1 is shocking and sad. Yet, with all this there is hope in this book. If you are up to the challenge, I ask you to hang in there and learn all you can about this disorder so you can help your family member get well and stay well.

For friends

You earn a special place in my heart because not many people stick around when their friend has bipolar 1. It is a very serious illness and can cause a lot of problems. You may have already experienced this for yourself.

It is difficult to understand what is going on in the mind of someone with bipolar 1 as it is such a complex disorder, but if you are keen to learn you will get a lot of help from this book.

Thank you for being a friend.

PART ONE
BIPOLAR BASICS

Chapter 1
What is bipolar disorder?

I shall begin by talking about bipolar disorder in general so you understand the illness and the difference between bipolar 1 and bipolar 2, then I shall move on to discuss bipolar 1 exclusively throughout the rest of the book. The discussion of bipolar 1 begins in chapter six. There we will cover the topic of what it is like to live with bipolar 1.

Bipolar disorder (formerly called manic–depression) is a mental illness that causes extreme shifts in mood, emotions, and energy. It also makes it difficult to think clearly, and often affects your ability to function normally in your everyday life.

Bipolar disorder is a physical disorder in that it affects the chemical balance in the brain, but it masquerades as a psychological disorder as it affects your behavior.

Mood swings

The mood swings in bipolar are cyclical in nature and can sometimes be predicted before they occur. Some people have regular mood cycles which makes them easier to manage. Other people cannot predict their mood cycles at all.

These episodes are called depression and mania, or hypomania. A depressive episode brings with it sadness, guilt, and suicidal ideation (thinking about suicide), whereas a manic, or hypomanic episode, causes elation or irritation. There is normally a euthymic period in between episodes where you can feel quite well without symptoms at all.

Of course, everybody has mood changes from one day to the next, but these changes are usually only present for a short period of time. Mood changes in bipolar disorder usually last longer and are far more severe.

Bipolar is a complex illness

Bipolar disorder is such a complex illness that it can be difficult to understand for the lay person. It is not made up of just mania and depression like some authorities would have you believe, but many different symptoms that are often disabling. We will talk about these in later chapters.

It must be said that bipolar disorder is not a character flaw or personality defect as some people believe. It cannot be controlled by will power, either. Many people do not understand this because they think it would be simple to learn how to control your emotions.

If you are talking to someone with this belief, you could explain to them that a person with diabetes cannot control the production of insulin by will power and you are not able to control your moods, either, due to chemical changes in your brain.

Diagnosing bipolar disorder

According to the DSM-5 (American Psychiatric Association's Diagnostic and Statistical Manual of Mental Disorders) bipolar 1 and 2 must meet the following criteria:

- Bipolar 1 – For bipolar 1, the person must have had at least one manic episode lasting a week or necessitating a hospital stay. Depressive episodes are not necessary for this diagnosis.

- Bipolar 2 – Bipolar 2 is diagnosed if a person has had at least one hypomanic episode and at least one major depressive episode.

Mania

To be considered bipolar 1 mania, the elevated, expansive, or irritable mood must last for at least one week and be present most of the day, nearly every day. To be considered hypomania, (as in bipolar 2) the mood must last for at least four consecutive days and be present most of the day, almost every day.

During this period, three or more of the following symptoms must be present in bipolar 1 mania, or bipolar 2 hypomania, and represent a significant change from your usual behavior:

- Inflated self-esteem or grandiosity
- Decreased need for sleep
- Increased talkativeness
- Racing thoughts
- Easily distracted
- Increase in goal-directed activity or psychomotor agitation
- Engagement in activities that hold the potential for painful consequences e.g., unrestrained buying sprees

Depression

The depressive side of bipolar disorder 1 and 2 is characterized by a major depressive episode resulting in a depressed mood and a loss of interest or pleasure in life. The DSM-5 states that a person must experience five or more of the following symptoms for two weeks to be diagnosed with a major depressive episode:

- Depressed mood most of the day, nearly every day
- Loss of interest or pleasure in all or almost all activities

- Significant weight loss or decrease, or increase in appetite

- Engaging in purposeless movements, such as pacing the room

- Fatigue or loss of energy

- Feelings of worthlessness or guilt

- Diminished ability to think or concentrate, or indecisiveness

- Recurrent thoughts of death and suicidal ideation, or a suicide attempt

Although Bipolar 2 is a form of bipolar disorder, it is different from bipolar 1 in that it has hypomania which is not as severe as mania. People with bipolar 2 are usually better able to function in society, and their mood swings do not require hospitalization.

Chapter 2
What is the incidence of bipolar disorder?

Bipolar disorder is present in approximately 5.7 million people and affects all ages, genders, races, ethnic groups, and social classes. It tends to run in families and is present in 80 – 90% of parents or sibling relatives. This makes it particularly difficult to decide whether to have children in a marriage.

Bipolar disorder generally appears around the late teens or early twenties, although it can appear later in life. Adults in their fifties and sixties have been diagnosed with bipolar disorder, but it is usually found that they have had this illness for some time but were never correctly diagnosed.

Some children also suffer from the illness, but it can be hard to diagnose bipolar disorder in children. It is very difficult to diagnose bipolar disorder in the teens because of the fluctuation of hormone levels and emotional highs and lows that are common. As a direct result of trauma, symptoms of other mental health conditions can also be found in children and teens.

Children do have episodes of major depression and mania (or hypomania) and the moods may shift rapidly, but it is difficult to diagnose bipolar disorder unless the shifts in mood are different from the child's normal moods.

Chapter 3
What is the cause of bipolar disorder?

⋘❈⋙

The cause of bipolar disorder is unknown, but it has been found in the following:

- An imbalance in brain chemistry: An alteration in brain chemistry is apparent in many mental illnesses, and medications given for this purpose have been shown to have a positive effect.

- A strong genetic link: bipolar disorder is present in many families, especially if a person has one or more parents with the disorder.

- Past traumas: This applies particularly to children who have lost a parent or have suffered the loss of a caretaker. It can also appear in families where childhood abuse has taken place.

However, all these possible causes are theories at the present time since none of them have been proved. Psychiatrists usually prescribe mood stabilizers when mood swings are present. They often see improvement in a person's symptoms, so it would follow that they attribute bipolar disorder to a chemical imbalance in the brain.

Stress, sleep disturbances, and self-abuse

Bipolar is also found in people who are undergoing a lot of stress, sleep disturbances, or take an excess of alcohol, or street drugs. But it is thought the illness had been present before the person had these difficulties.

If left untreated, bipolar can worsen with age and the incidence of suicide in both manic and depressive cycles is high. About one in five people with bipolar will commit suicide, and it is the tenth leading cause of death in America.

Bipolar is a lifelong disorder and cannot be cured at the present time. However, it responds well to treatment such as medication, psychotherapy, lifestyle changes, and support groups.

Chapter 4
What illnesses are similar to bipolar disorder?

In order to manage and treat bipolar disorder properly a correct diagnosis must be made, but according to the National Depressive and Manic-Depressive Association, 69% of patients are initially misdiagnosed. A third of these patients remain undiagnosed for ten years or more. There are no blood tests, MRIs or CT scans that can be used to test for bipolar disorder at the present time.

Several illnesses resemble bipolar disorder, but your psychiatrist should give you a physical on your first visit to rule them out. Sometimes the symptoms overlap, and patients may have co-existing illnesses, especially psychiatric ones.

The common physical illnesses that are sometimes diagnosed as bipolar disorder include the following:

- Thyroid disease
- Lupus
- HIV
- Syphilis
- Other infections

In addition to this, many psychiatric conditions resemble bipolar disorder making it even harder to get an accurate diagnosis. The following is not an exhaustive list but will give you some idea of the many illnesses that can be mistaken for bipolar disorder.

The psychiatric diseases that are often misdiagnosed as bipolar disorder are:

- Unipolar depression (major depressive disorder)
- BPD (borderline personality disorder)
- ADHD (attention deficit hyper-activity disorder)
- Schizophrenia
- Substance abuse

Is it major depressive disorder (unipolar depression)?

It is quite easy to differentiate between unipolar and bipolar disorder because people with unipolar disorder do not have hypomania or mania. They are both mood disorders, but quite different.

Bipolar disorder is often misdiagnosed as major depressive disorder at first because people generally report depression when they feel ill, and the low mood interferes with their everyday life. Then, when their depression worsens, they go to see their doctor for medication or other help.

Bipolar disorder used to be called manic-depression. Depressive episodes in major depressive disorder are similar to bipolar depressive episodes.

Quite often the clinician does not suspect bipolar disorder because the person does not always remember to report their symptoms correctly. If hypomanic or manic episodes took place in the distant past, it is easy to forget all about them. The person may have been what they think of as extra happy or irritable, but they have not equated that with illness, so they don't think to mention it to the doctor.

None-the-less, it is always wise to report an incident such as this so that a true diagnosis can be made. Sometimes a relative or friend will be able to remember an incident or two that the person has forgotten.

Occasionally, somebody is given an anti-depressant for a depressive episode, and in some cases, it triggers a manic or hypomanic reaction. This would then change the diagnosis from major depressive disorder to bipolar disorder.

Is it BPD (borderline personality disorder)?

This personality disorder has several symptoms that are similar to bipolar disorder, but the two are very different illnesses each requiring different treatment.

Both have unstable mood episodes and self-destructive behavior on occasion. However, the mood episodes with borderline personality disorder tend to change rapidly throughout the day and are usually in response to everyday life issues.

People with bipolar disorder generally have longer mood episodes unless they have rapid cycling where the mood changes frequently. Their episodes can be a response to everyday life issues, or quite spontaneous.

Some people have borderline personality disorder as well as bipolar disorder.

Is it ADHD
(attention deficit hyperactivity disorder)?

ADHD is a common illness characterized by impulsive behavior, forgetfulness, negative self-image, lack of motivation, and restlessness. It is essential that a correct diagnosis be made in order to properly treat this condition. ADHD symptoms usually appear in childhood whereas bipolar symptoms usually appear in late teens or early adulthood. People with rapid cycling bipolar disorder in adulthood often had ADHD in their teens.

Is it schizophrenia?

Although both conditions start in early adulthood, these two illnesses differ in that bipolar is a mood disorder whereas schizophrenia is a psychotic disorder. This means that people with bipolar disorder have manic and depressive moods that cycle and often begin and end abruptly. Psychotic symptoms in schizophrenia may last a long time, even with the help of anti-psychotic medication.

However, the confusion comes when people with bipolar 1 have psychotic episodes arising from severe depression or mania. These episodes closely resemble those of schizophrenia. However, bipolar psychosis is temporary and only lasts as long as the mood persists.

While anti-psychotics may help both conditions, Lithium, (a mood-stabilizer) is usually more helpful to people with bipolar disorder than to people with schizophrenia.

Is it substance abuse?

Excessive use of alcohol and/or drugs can make a bipolar diagnosis more difficult to treat. People who have substance abuse are often unaware of their actions, and elation or irritability can easily resemble a manic episode. If a person does have bipolar as well as substance abuse these two conditions are diagnosed as dual-diagnosis. This is very common indeed.

The use of alcohol or drugs to self-medicate makes bipolar more difficult to treat.

Chapter 5
What are the effects on the family?

Bipolar has a considerable effect on family life because it affects your behavior as well as your energy level. When you are depressed, your family must learn to accept your behavior and that can be very difficult. People who have never been depressed are sometimes unable to empathize and want to blame you for your illness.

They will say all kinds of things that are upsetting and make you feel more depressed. They often suggest things you could do to get well that are impossible to do when you are in a deep depression. If this kind of talk persists, you can tell them you would gladly do the things they suggest if you were able.

Then when you are manic, it has a really big effect on your family, and can cause an enormous amount of stress for everybody. Most people can understand depression to a degree, but mania is very different. There is no logic behind manic behavior which is very difficult to accept.

Your mood swings can be exhausting for caretakers who usually only want the best for you. The results for the family may be:

- Extreme emotional reactions like guilt, grief, and worry

- Disruptions to the family routine

- Financial stress

- Strained family relationships

- Difficulty maintaining relationships in and outside the family setting

Bipolar can have a significant impact on friends. People you have known for years may not remain friends with you when they hear of your diagnosis. If you are lucky, others may stand by you. That is good because you need a great deal of support when you have bipolar.

We will discuss these topics more in a later chapter.

Chapter 6
What is it like to live with bipolar 1 disorder?

Now that you know the facts about bipolar disorder in general, we can talk about bipolar 1 disorder exclusively. I will only be referring to bipolar 1 from now on in this book.

You will find that stigma associated with bipolar disorder, especially bipolar 1, is alive and well and will likely influence you throughout your life. The only thing to do when you are faced with this problem is to either avoid mentioning it altogether or educate people about bipolar. Educating people is fine in theory, but you will find that many people do not want to learn about bipolar and are afraid that it is contagious in some way. It is sad that people think this way, but in the end, we must accept their feelings.

You may want to diminish the stigma by being open about your bipolar disorder, and that is up to you. It will be received by some and not others. You should be aware of that.

When you have bipolar 1, you have extreme fluctuations in mood — mania (abnormally happy or irritable), and de-pression (sad and hopeless) – that typically last for days or weeks. These mood swings may occur rarely or frequently.

On occasion, some people suffer mood fluctuations for many months or years while others rarely have mood swings at all.

It will be noted that even though depression is common, it is not necessary for a diagnosis of bipolar 1.

Mania

The manic cycles that are found in bipolar 1 are particularly difficult to live with and can often be so severe as to require hospitalization. If you have bipolar 1 you will no doubt have said and done many things you regret when you were having a manic episode.

This is a very upsetting side of the illness as it causes many relationship break ups. As I said before, it is common for people's family and friends to disappear when they know you have bipolar 1 disorder which is a very good reason for choosing wisely who you tell about your illness.

Depression

Depression in bipolar 1 can be debilitating, necessitating time away from your normal activities. This is very upsetting for most people, and the lack of motivation to do anything can make you even more depressed.

As you will know, if you have long depressive episodes, the feelings of hopelessness, guilt, and worthlessness are particularly difficult to live with. When you get really low, it seems as if there is no way out of the depression.

It is hard to understand that *"this too shall pass"* when you are in the depths of despair. However, depression does pass, and you can remind yourself of this fact by writing down what you are normally like when you are not depressed. Then look at your list when you are ill and you will be able to see that you are not the depression, it is just another symptom of bipolar 1. You are perfectly fine when you are well.

In fact, it is good to remember that you are not bipolar, you are a person with bipolar disorder. This illness is totally distinct from your everyday, euthymic (normal) personality.

Psychosis

As I have said, when you have bipolar 1 you can also suffer from psychosis. In fact, over half of the people with bipolar 1 will suffer psychosis at some point in their lives. This will no doubt be very disturbing for you and your family because there is no logical explanation for the symptoms. It is pointless trying to rationalize with someone when they are psychotic. When in a psychotic episode, you will often need to be hospitalized.

Bipolar 1 with mixed features

This is a particularly distressing mood as it means you have symptoms of both mania and depression at the same time. This needs specialized treatment.

Rapid cycling

People with rapid cycling, suffer mood fluctuations at least four times a year, and some even have rapidly changing mood episodes throughout the day or week. Rapid cycling is very difficult to treat.

Euthymic period

In between cycles you may experience a euthymic period, which is more like your normal mood when you are well. Some people experience emotional highs and lows during this euthymic period but not enough to be classed as a mood swing.

Work and relationships often suffer when you have bipolar 1 disorder. Many relationships have been destroyed, and jobs have been lost to this illness.

Summing it up

We now know that bipolar disorder is a very complex illness that affects many different things in your life. So far, we have examined the following topics:

- The diagnosis of bipolar disorder
- The incidence
- The cause
- Similar illnesses
- How it effects family life
- What it is like to live with bipolar 1

Family and friends

Imagine that you are at the beginning of a journey and that journey is going to teach you how to cope with your friend or relative who has bipolar 1 disorder. This can be a very tall order as so many problems can arise. You may have the best intentions in the world, but they could easily backfire on you as the mood swings in bipolar 1 are often unpredictable and painful.

Learn all you can about the illness. Strive to become an expert. You can read many articles online, buy books, or take them out of the library. There are many support groups for patients, relatives and friends who are going through the same thing. You may find it very helpful to attend one of these groups and share your stories. Also, most support groups will help you learn more about bipolar 1.

See if you can participate in making a crisis plan with your loved one when they are well. Discuss beforehand where they would like to go if they are admitted to the hospital for treatment. Also, list phone numbers of support-ers and the medications they are taking. We will talk more about a crisis plan later in this book.

If you have a friend with bipolar, I hope this book will be of help to you. Your friend is lucky to have you as they will need all the support they can get.

For now, I am happy that you are reading this book because it will undoubtedly help you on your journey.

PART TWO
THE SYMPTOMS OF BIPOLAR 1

Chapter 7
Symptoms of mania

As we have already discussed, only people with bipolar 1 have true mania. People with bipolar 2 have hypomania which is difficult to live with but doesn't usually have a negative effect on the person's ability to function.

Also, people with bipolar 2 do not have to go to the hospital with hypomania as it never reaches the heights of mania. If it should turn into mania, the person will be given a diagnosis of bipolar 1.

People with bipolar 1 mania have symptoms that often prevent them from being productive and living their life to the fullest. The symptoms of mania soon become unmanageable and out of control.

Before I got my bipolar disorder under control, I had difficulty writing anything, but have now completed two full-length books. It just shows you what is possible if you have patience with bipolar medications and lifestyle. We shall be talking much more about these things in the following chapters.

Most people feel very happy when things are going well for them. They may have won a prize, or got married, or had a baby, but just feeling happy is not mania. That is purely a positive reaction to life's events.

Mania brings with it a sense of omnipotence, a feeling of all's right with the world, and you have never been happier in your life. You are also convinced that you can do anything you put your mind to and will take enormous risks that you would never consider taking when you are well.

At first, bipolar mania may allow you to be productive, but soon enough it will get out of hand if nothing is done to intervene. Then it can become unmanageable and lead to hospitalization.

The early stages of mania.

You may find that the early stages of mania allow you to complete tasks you would not normally be able to do, especially if you are just emerging from a depressive episode.

It is very common in the first stages of mania to complete jobs you don't usually have the motivation for. Then, of course, the mania sets in, and projects get started and never finished. Before you know it, you have piles of things all around you and nothing gets accomplished.

I used to get highly motivated when manic and completed a lot of DIY jobs around the house. One time I painted all my kitchen cabinets. Never again. That was a full-time job. But I did it and was grateful to have had the opportunity.

Does mania affect your energy?

You are generally not tired at all when you are manic. It is one thing to be tired and unable to sleep – this is called insomnia which is prevalent in depression – but to find sleeping a waste of time is another thing entirely.

Sorting out cupboards or scrubbing the grout in the kitchen tiles at three in the morning is possible during bipolar mania. Many people find they suddenly have an enormous amount of energy, so the tasks they may have been putting off for a very long time are finally tackled.

I used to sort cupboards in the middle of the night when manic. Seeing as I live alone, it was not a problem because I wasn't disturbing anyone, but I would have done better with more sleep.

One thing I have noticed that seems peculiar to mania is that the world, and everybody in it, seems to be moving too slowly, and you don't understand why things don't speed up. If you have experienced mania, you will probably have noticed that for yourself.

How does mania affect creativity?

Mania can affect your creativity and that is why many creative people don't want to take bipolar medications. Many projects get started during the first few days or weeks of mania. But whether these projects get completed or not is another issue entirely because, as the mania progresses, you usually become very confused and erratic in your thinking.

One aspect of a manic episode is you think all your creative endeavors are wonderful, but many people are disappointed when they are well because they can see their creations are not wonderful at all.

How does mania affect relationships?

You are often good company in the first stages of mania because you are interesting and expansive in your ideas. People like being around you, and your organizational skills are apparent. People at work are happy to help you.

However, this situation is short lived when mania progresses, and the ideas come thick and fast. The speech becomes very loud and grates on other people's nerves. Being around somebody who is talking fast and loudly interrupting your every word soon becomes very annoying. People will begin to avoid you.

As the mania progresses, the thoughts become more and more disorganized, and you go off at tangents that are unrelated to the conversation. This is when people start to get alarmed and either ignore you or try to help.

It is not easy to help a person when they don't want to be helped and, if you are manic, you will not think you are ill at all. If you have never felt better in your life, the reasoning is how can you possibly be ill? It makes no sense.

Here are a few symptoms of mania that you may recognize in yourself:

- Racing thoughts
- Loud, fast, disorganized speech
- Feeling omnipotent, elated, and superior to the average person
- Unable to sleep, or needing very little sleep
- Being very productive and creative
- Having many projects on the go at once, but being unable to finish them
- Feeling angry, and having episodes of rage
- Starting arguments with people
- Taking unnecessary risks like over-spending, speeding, making unwise business decisions, and having promiscuous and unprotected sex with strangers
- Loss of inhibitions
- Having obsessions like an overwhelming interest in the occult or religion

As you can see, this is not a normal way to behave, but it seems perfectly normal when you are manic. You will likely resent anyone who tries to calm you down and rebel against authorities that want you to take medication or go into the hospital. But that is how an episode of mania often ends.

One of the major problems with mania is that you harm relationships with people who are close to you. Many things are said in the throes of mania that are sorely regretted later, but it is often too late, and you may not be forgiven.

Bipolar is the relationship destroyer. Most people have a string of broken relationships that lie in their wake. I lost most of my friends to this disease. As soon as they heard I had bipolar, they disappeared. I lost the ones that stuck around, too, as I kept picking arguments with them.

It should be noted here that not all mania is good, and not everybody feels omnipotent. Many people have dysphoric mania where they get very irritable and angry. This leads to agitation and being out of control.

Agitation is a very unpleasant feeling, and you think you need to be moving and doing things all the time. Sometimes, this will be purposeless like pacing up and down. Other people keep getting up and walking about, going from room to room but accomplishing nothing.

What are the causes of mania?

Bipolar 1 mania often comes out of nowhere, with no explanation. It can follow a bout of depression which initially makes it very welcome. But mania soon escalates out of control and the person is on a one-way ride to disaster.

It is thought that mania is purely chemical in nature as there is no doubt that when you have bipolar you have a chemical imbalance in your brain. However, sleeplessness and late nights do seem to contribute to mania and should be controlled if possible.

How important is sleep in preventing mania?

Sleep is very important to bipolar stability. Without a regular sleep routine, people with bipolar often succumb to episodes of depression or mania even if only a couple of night's sleep are interrupted. The problem is that sleep doesn't always come easily in bipolar 1 and many people have trouble sticking to routines. This lack of sleep can cause problems for you, so it is always wise to do what you can to sleep for seven to nine hours each night. Some people can only sleep for three to five hours a night, and this seems to prolong the mania.

People who stay out late at parties are particularly susceptible to mania and drinking alcohol in excess can cause a disruption in sleep patterns as well. Unfortunately, it can cause problems between friends because other people don't always realize why it is important for you to get regular sleep. But if you do not insist on going to bed at your regular bedtime, you will likely become sick with bipolar mania after a short time.

Does travel have anything to do with mania?

Yes, it has been found that if you travel to different time zones, it is quite likely that it will interrupt your regular sleep pattern. This can bring on a manic episode (or a depressive episode) and cause you a lot of problems if you are on holiday or at a business meeting.

I used to have a lot of trouble with time zones when visiting my brother in Australia. Trying to stick to a regular medication regimen when you are gaining sixteen hours in flight is nearly impossible. I never knew whether to take my morning medications in the evening, or not. And by the time I got to Sydney, I was quite confused and well on my way to mania or depression.

The only thing I have tried is to space out my medications as if I am taking them morning and evening and this sometimes works. I also take many other medications for physical problems, so I use this rule of thumb when taking those as well. But it is not ideal, and I can sometimes slip up. In that case, I must force myself to sleep for a few hours as soon as I get to my brother's house in the hopes of allaying a manic or depressive episode. I have had some dreadful holidays due to bipolar 1 disorder.

Does stress cause mania?

There is evidence that an increase in stress, or experiencing stress for a long period of time, does sometimes precipitate a manic episode. However, it is often because many people lose sleep during a stressful time. When you have bipolar 1, you should avoid stress as much as possible.

What do you do if you feel a manic episode coming on?

Unfortunately, mania often sneaks up on you and, before you know it, it is too late to do anything about it. That is why it is an advantage to have someone help you with this problem. If they see mania is on the horizon, they can encourage you to see the doctor and get a temporary medication change. Once mania has set it, it is very hard to go back to where you were when you were well.

The prodromal effects of mania

The prodromal period is when the initial symptoms appear before the full-blown effects of mania.

Although mania can build quickly, you may find that you have prodromal symptoms leading up to mania weeks or even months ahead of time, so you are more likely to be able to avert an episode. However, it is common to disregard the symptoms of the prodrome altogether, then you are surprised when you have a full-blown manic episode.

Here are some prodromal symptoms to look out for:

Elevated mood
You may start out feeling in a very good mood and think there is nothing wrong with you. You may feel invincible and more confident than usual. That is why it helps to have someone else around as you won't notice it as a problem. Friends and relatives can help spot the problem and suggest you get treatment.

Decreased need for sleep
You may start finding that you have less need for sleep and are up at all hours of the night sorting out cupboards and drawers.

Increased interest in activities
People in the prodromal stage of mania often find an interest in studying something in minute detail, like religion or the occult, and they find they feel sexually aroused much of the time.

Volatility. You may lose your temper at the least little thing

Unfortunately, it is only in retrospect, after the full-blown manic episode has subsided, that you can see these symptoms for what they are. It can be helpful to ask a family member or friend to write these things down while they are happening. This may avert a manic episode at another time.

If you, or somebody else, should notice the prodromal symptoms of mania, that would be the time for a doctor to adjust your mood-stabilizer. Never ever adjust or stop your medication on your own. This can make you very sick.

Chapter 8
Symptoms of depression

It is true that you don't need to have had depressive episodes to be diagnosed with bipolar 1, but it is also true that many people do in fact suffer with depression. This can be disabling for days, weeks, or even months, especially if the right treatment is not obtained.

I personally had far more depression with my bipolar 1 diagnosis than I had mania, and it got worse as I grew older. Bipolar disorder has a habit of getting worse with age, unfortunately. This is especially true if you do not seek early treatment.

Is bipolar depression different from unipolar depression?

Depression in bipolar is said to be the same as it is in major depressive disorder in so much as the symptoms are similar, but it does not generally last as long which is a blessing. People with major depressive disorder often have depression for many months, if not years, and medication only takes the edge off it.

If you start to feel sad and empty, and you have a bipolar 1 diagnosis, it is important that you see a doctor as soon as possible to adjust your medication.

I have found that when you have bipolar 1, you can sink into the abyss of despair in a matter of a couple of days. I could wake up feeling suicidal in the morning for no particular reason at all. This happened frequently after manic episodes. As soon as the fun of mania subsided, I would fall into a deep depression which would last for a week, or so. I suppose I can be grateful that it didn't last any longer, and it didn't end in suicide which is very possible with bipolar 1 depression.

What is your view of depression?

The way I think of depression is suddenly finding myself at the bottom of a deep, dark well. The walls are caked in slippery mud. There is no light above as the sky is black, and there is no way I can see of getting out of the well. I try to climb the walls, but they are too slick, and I sink back down to the bottom of the well in despair.

That to me is depression, but you will have your own interpretation. Whichever way you look at it, depression is hell, and it is very difficult to live with.

Another thing I noticed when I was depressed is that I was suddenly stripped of all energy, and I could hardly make it across the room. I spent my days going from bed to chair and chair to bed, and my nights lying awake worrying that the depression would never pass.

When you are depressed, it is very difficult to see an end to it. You feel so hopeless that you lose all incentive to get well. Your motivation to do anything is just not there. Even the everyday things like taking a shower or brushing your teeth become such enormous tasks you think you will never be able to accomplish them.

Then the feelings of guilt, sadness and worthlessness descend upon you. You think you are to blame for all the troubles in your family and indeed the world. You take the blame for everything. If you are normally low in self-esteem, you begin to feel that nobody cares about you even if you have a loving family.

You may have trouble sleeping, or you may sleep too much. Sometimes, I think you need to sleep a lot to let the body heal because the body is affected as well as the mind. People get all kinds of aches and pains with depression.

Suddenly, all pleasure is drained from the things you used to love to do, and you can find no enjoyment in anything at all. Even eating is not pleasurable. You eat to fill yourself up, or you don't eat at all. Losing more than 5% of your normal body weight is a sign of deep depression.

I always found that I would cry a lot in depression. Not for any reason, and half the time I didn't even know I was crying at all. Once, I went to see a doctor for something completely unrelated to bipolar disorder and he asked me why I was crying. I hadn't been aware that I was, but when I thought about it, I could feel the tears coursing down my cheeks. He doubled the dose of my mood stabilizer there and then. It worked, and I got better.

Some people do not feel sad, worthless, or guilty, they don't feel anything at all. This can be terribly distressing. Instead of feeling like a member of the human race, you start to think you are empty inside and don't exist at all.

I had this happen to me once when I went on another visit to see my brother in Australia. I had a big problem with taking my medications at the right time on the plane and was sick the whole month I was there. When we parted at the airport, I remember riding up the escalator and feeling nothing at all. I could see him standing there, but it was as if I didn't even know him.

I was so depressed I couldn't engage for the whole journey home. In fact, I was so sick that when I arrived in Sydney to change flights, I thought I was already in Texas. The stewardess was completely baffled and told me we hadn't left Australia yet.

What is the worst that can happen?

In my opinion, the very worst part of depression is the feeling of wanting to die. I always used to wish I was dead because I couldn't see the point in living. What was there to live for if you can't get out of the black hole?

This is when the planning for suicide begins. Nearly every-body does it because wishing you were dead is merely a symptom of bipolar depression. Most people get very alarmed by this situation because they do not really want to die, they just don't want to live like that anymore. But thinking of death and dying is all part of bipolar depression.

If you think about it, you will be able to see that it is just another symptom to contend with.

My therapist told me something one day that I have never forgotten. He said, *"Suicide is not an option."* I had to think about that, but always remembered it when I was at death's door. It is not an option for you either.

It is very important to prevent suicide by calling:

The National Suicide Prevention Hotline: 1 800-273-8255

Even if you don't feel you have reached the end of the road, they will be pleased to talk to you and listen to your problems. I have spent many hours talking on the phone to these kind volunteers. They were always willing to listen and give me advice.

Keep all dangerous things like knives, guns and medication hidden away if you are feeling very depressed. Get somebody to take care of them, so you won't be tempted to use them.

Bipolar disorder can be a fatal disease. It has a very high suicidal rate with approximately one person in five who go on to kill themselves. Many more make suicide attempts. Be sure to talk to someone about this before you do something rash.

Make certain they understand you are seriously thinking of killing yourself as some people prefer not to believe it and brush it off lightly. But this is a very important issue which needs to be discussed with someone you can trust.

One thing that is fortunate is that when you are deeply depressed you do not usually have the energy or motivation to kill yourself. It is only when you are coming out of your depression that you find you are ready to carry out your plan. It is then that you need to take action to make sure you don't do something that would not be an answer to your problem. Remember it would cause much heartache and guilt to those who love you.

My husband killed himself (he didn't have bipolar) and it took me many years to recover from the anger.

Don't do it.

Should I go to the hospital?

People with bipolar 1 are often admitted to the hospital when they are deeply depressed. Everybody has their own experiences with psychiatric hospitals. Either you think it is a nice restful atmosphere, or it is a place where you lose your identity. Either way, many people with bipolar 1 depression are admitted to the hospital to find a medication cocktail that works for them.

Once, when I was severely depressed, I was admitted to a hospital and slept for six days straight. I just got up to go to the bathroom, then got straight back into bed and went to sleep again. I hardly ate or drank a thing. Finally, the doctor told me it was time I got up and participated with group therapy in the unit, so I did.

I remember that feeling of being so drained of energy I could hardly stand up. In fact, two junior nurses had to give me a shower because I couldn't balance on my own.

That is an example of very severe depression when all hope is lost. I do hope you never have to experience that as it is very frightening.

You might like to check off some symptoms of depression that you have had yourself:

- Depressed mood, feeling sad, hopeless, and guilty for no reason

- Marked loss of interest in most things

- No motivation to do anything.

- Either sleeping too little (insomnia) or sleeping too much (hypersomnia)

- Either eating too little or eating too much

- Extreme fatigue

- Feelings of worthlessness and shame

- Decreased ability to concentrate or make decisions

- Thinking about death and dying

If you can check off five or more of these symptoms right now, you will need to see your doctor and get treatment right away.

Chapter 9
Symptoms of psychosis

Psychosis affects more than 50% of people with bipolar 1. Psychosis and mania are what sets the illness apart from bipolar 2. If you have bipolar 1, you can become psychotic with a manic or a depressive episode if your mood swings are severe enough. These episodes are called mood-congruent or mood-incongruent depending on whether, or not, they match your mood at the time.

If you are depressed, you might believe that you are a scourge on the face of the earth, whereas if you are manic, you might have grandiose thoughts and believe you are a famous person, or extremely wealthy.

Psychosis means losing touch with reality

As I have said before, when this happens, it is hard to tell the difference between bipolar psychosis and schizophrenia as they both have similar symptoms. What makes them stand apart is that people with schizophrenia have long bouts of psychosis that are not always relieved by medication, whereas people with bipolar 1 are not psychotic all the time as psychotic symptoms are usually temporary.

The symptoms of psychosis are:

Hallucinations
These are when you see, hear, smell, feel, and taste things that are not there, and are not experienced by other people. You may well see strange sights or hear music playing. Or you might hear people screaming, or smell smoke.

Delusions
False beliefs that persist in the face of evidence against them. They can be persecutory, grandiose, obsessive, or jealous. It is common to think people are plotting against you, or your partner is unfaithful, or you become obsessed with religion or the occult.

Disorganized thinking
This is when your thoughts are not clear and you jump from topic to topic, talking in riddles so nobody can understand you.

Psychosis is generally very frightening for the person experiencing it. Although you might accept that strange things are real, at the same time you are very frightened because you seem to be the only one experiencing them. If you ask for validation from others, they will try to convince you that your hallucinations and delusions are not real. This becomes very confusing indeed and sets you apart from the rest of the world. It is as if other people have secret that they are hiding from you.

It is this loneliness that causes so much fear when you have psychosis. You have an uneasy feeling that things are not quite right, but you can't put your finger on it. This leaves you agitated and anxious.

Sleep does not come easily when you are psychotic. You can toss and turn and worry about what is going on inside your head all night. Eating sometimes becomes difficult, especially if you have strange tastes like metal or blood in your mouth. And hygiene suffers. When you have psychosis, you lose interest in the things that everybody else takes for granted.

I have been psychotic more times than I can remember and can vouch for the fact that it is a very lonely place to be. I have seen people with horns coming out of their head (even my psychiatrist!), smelled smoke, heard my voice being called, had voices talking to me out of my computer, felt bugs crawling all over me, and many more things besides. It is alarming, I can tell you.

I was also convinced that my best friend was trying to kill me, at one time, and drove to the police station at three in the morning to get help. I gave them a list of all the things I thought she had done, and told them she had just been to my house knocking on the door in the middle of the night. They took me to her house, to verify my accusations, and felt the hood of her car. It was stone cold, but I still believed she had been trying to kill me. Nothing they could have said would have changed my mind.

That episode ended with a month in the hospital and many medication changes.

Chapter 10
Mixed features

Some people have what is called bipolar 1 with mixed features. This variation used to be called bipolar 1 with, "mixed episodes" but this has since been renamed. These episodes include symptoms of both depression and mania that are experienced at the same time and are very uncomfortable to live with.

You may feel extremely sad and worthless, yet at the same time, feel agitated with racing thoughts and confusion. Many people experience immense joy one minute, then they are suicidal with depression the next.

This is a variation of bipolar 1 disorder which is very difficult to treat. However, it must be addressed to avoid hospital admission. Your psychiatrist will often treat the mania and the depression at the same time and, as you can imagine, this is a very skilled job with much room for error.

Bipolar disorder with mixed features is more likely to cause frequent mood episodes, and they can sometimes resist treatment altogether. They can also last much longer than normal mood episodes.

There is a lot of work being done on this at the moment, as some people believe that far more episodes with mixed features exist in bipolar than are recognized.

Chapter 11
Rapid cycling

Some people have bipolar episodes that are months or years apart, but others are unfortunate enough to have more than four episodes of mania, depression, or psychosis in one year. This is called rapid cycling.

It is even possible to have cycles from depression to mania or from mania to depression every day, sometimes from hour to hour which is very exhausting for the person and very confusing for the family.

If you should have four changes in mood a month, that is called ultra-rapid cycling. These cycles are often temporary but occur more frequently in women.

Treatment is with medication and talk therapy. It might also be helpful to track your moods on a bipolar mood tracker that you can find online. Sleep is also good for rapid cycling. It helps to get your normal, euthymic mood back again.

Summing it up

We have covered a lot of ground here, but I hope it was helpful and that you recognized your symptoms on these pages. As we shall see later, there are many ways of dealing with these symptoms, and I hope you will try some of them.

So far, we have covered:

- Bipolar 1 mania.
- Bipolar 1 depression.
- Bipolar 1 psychosis.
- Bipolar 1 with mixed features.
- Bipolar 1 with rapid cycling.

Family and friends

Helping someone in mania is very difficult because they do not want to be helped as they do not think they are sick. Try slowing them down in the initial stages and get them to rest if you are unable to get them to sleep. People are very uncooperative in mania, and it is difficult to get them to do what you want. If the mania escalates and gets out of control, leave them alone. Let them calm down while you get on with your life. If things get really unmanageable, you may have to take them to the hospital, or call 911, for their own safety and yours.

Many horrible things are said and done in mania, and the person may well forget about them afterwards. It is very unfortunate that there is this side to mania as it can cause rifts in even the best relationships. I know it is sometimes difficult to forgive, and that must be your choice.

People with depression are more receptive to intervention because they feel very sick indeed. If you intervene in the early stages, you may be able to get help and slow the progression of the episode. Make sure they are getting medical attention so they can start on a course of treatment as it often takes several weeks for medications to work.

Be kind to someone in depression. It is an illness, and they are not to blame for their mood swings. No amount of badgering, pleading, or berating will get them to snap out of it. It is not possible to snap out of depression. Rest assured, if people were capable of healing themselves, they would have done so already.

People in psychosis are very difficult to handle. It is no good trying to convince them that their beliefs are false because they will only get more agitated. Do not argue with them or try to change their opinions. Delusions are very real in psychosis, and the beliefs are unshakable. Again, seek help from the medical profession.

If you think your loved one has mixed features or rapid cycling, it is imperative they receive care immediately.

PART THREE
COMPLICATIONS
OF BIPOLAR 1

Chapter 12
Anxiety

Anxiety is very prevalent in bipolar 1 disorder. Over half the people with bipolar 1 also have some form of anxiety disorder. This complicates your life immeasurably as bipolar is bad enough to have to deal with without the added symptoms of anxiety.

The presence of an anxiety disorder complicates the treatment of bipolar and can make it worse. These illnesses are generalized anxiety disorder (GAD), social anxiety, obsessive compulsive disorder (OCD), post-traumatic stress disorder (PTSD), and others.

Children are often diagnosed with both bipolar disorder and anxiety disorder. The anxiety usually comes first, then the bipolar disorder at a later stage. When these comorbidities (more than one diagnosis) occur, children and young people in general are more at risk of substance abuse and suicide, so great care must be taken to ensure that the diagnosis and treatment are correct.

Because comorbid anxiety disorders can worsen the course of bipolar, it is best if the doctor screens for both conditions regularly.

It is impossible to describe what anxiety feels like to people who have never experienced it. If it becomes a regular occurrence, it can take over your every waking moment. Many people live with anxiety on a daily basis.

What are the symptoms of anxiety disorder?

- Restlessness
- Constant worry
- Exhaustion
- Difficulty in focusing on any subject
- Body tension
- Insomnia
- Racing heartbeat
- Hyperventilating
- Irritability
- A feeling of being unable to balance

If you look carefully at this list of symptoms, you will see that some of them resemble bipolar mood swings. In mania, you are susceptible to restlessness, difficulty in focusing, irritability, and insomnia. Then in depression, all these symptoms can be present. For that reason, it can be difficult for the doctor to come to a correct diagnosis. He must tease apart each symptom and decide which is anxiety and which is bipolar disorder.

However, if you have anxiety, you will definitely know the difference between that and bipolar 1. I can tell the difference, but it is very hard to describe how I feel to a doctor.

Sometimes, it is only when you have all these symptoms of anxiety that a diagnosis of bipolar 1 can be made. When this occurs, the treatment will be different. So, it is imperative that the doctor knows how you are feeling.

Before taking strong medications, it is highly advisable to try therapy first: Cognitive Behavioral Therapy (CBT), family or couples therapy, or psychotherapy may be of help.

Many medications are very addictive, or habit forming, and can only be taken for a short period of time, so it is far better to engage in other strategies or seek therapy.

What can you do to stop anxiety?

Here are a few things which may help:

- Relaxation exercises
- Meditation
- Yoga / tai chi / qigong
- Getting out of the house
- Advocating for yourself to get what you need

Anxiety is exhausting to live with every day. What would seem like a simple task, can take far longer to complete, and cause much worry. Even getting dressed and making breakfast before you go to work can take an enormous effort, leaving you feeling drained. Then if you are able to work, every hour of the day is a marathon to be undertaken.

When I had a lot of anxiety, I used to shake all over, and my palms used to sweat. I was nursing at the time and had great difficulty doing my job. As I oversaw the unit, I had many people reporting to me, and the anxiety made me very nervous about keeping the unit running smoothly. Even speaking to the doctors was nerve-wracking.

I used to have dreadful anxiety when on the telephone and that was a big part of my job. I also had a problem with writing and signing my name in front of other people. I used to wait until they were busy before writing anything down. This was in the days before computers were used in hospitals, and there was a lot of writing to be done about the patient's condition. This brought me out in a sweat and my hands visibly trembled.

If you have anxiety, you will no doubt understand how difficult it is to work. Many people must take time off, and many jobs have been lost to anxiety.

I had anxiety for several years and decided long ago that I would face my fears. To do this, I had to change my way of thinking and take on new challenges.

Once I stepped out of my comfort zone, I was able to put most of my anxiety behind me. The best way to do this, I found, was to go on holiday on my own. I went to Australia three times, England, Malta, and Costa Rica, and by the time I had done that my anxiety was much better. I did have some difficult times on my own, there is no denying that, but overall, I now feel that I can cope with most things in life.

I also took a course in public speaking. I was totally paralyzed at first and could hardly get a word out, let alone speak for five minutes. I found five minutes was a very long time indeed, but I did it.

These are some suggestions you might like to try, but if they are not possible, try stepping out of your comfort zone in a small way so that you can cure your anxiety forever.

I am sure that by reading this book, you will be able to cope better with your anxiety. You must practice most of the suggestions I have laid out for you though, or you will not progress.

If you are totally unable to cure your anxiety with self-help techniques or therapy, you will need help with medication in order to lead a productive life.

Chapter 13
Panic attacks

If you have ever had a panic attack, you won't need me to tell you how terrifying it is. I have had many panic attacks in my life and have been overcome with fear every time.

When you have a panic attack, you have some or all of the following symptoms:

- Feeling as if you are going mad or going to die
- Terror and dread
- Heart banging
- Racing heartbeat
- Shortness of breath
- Feeling faint
- Nausea
- Chest pain
- Trembling
- Sweaty palms
- Chills
- Hot flashes

- Choking sensation
- Dry mouth
- Pins and needles
- Churning stomach
- Feeling of wanting to go to the bathroom
- Feeling of not being connected to the body

Panic attacks are caused by the fight or flight mechanism. Adrenaline is pumped into the body so that you can run away. This was very useful in the days when cave men used to ward off lions. They either fought the beast, or they ran away. But today, in the world we live in, this reaction is no longer appropriate.

Unfortunately, instead of staying calm, my immediate reaction to a panic attack was to run as fast as I could to get away from the situation, which obviously does not go down too well in many circumstances.

At nursing school, when they showed a film of a funeral, I ran out of the room gasping for air when the casket disappeared behind the curtain. This scene brought back terrible memories of when my mother died. It was amazing that my tutor, who was a nurse, didn't understand what was happening to me when I tried to explain it to her.

Do people go to the hospital with a panic attack?

I have been to the emergency room twice with panic attacks because I thought I was having a heart attack. This is very common. When you arrive, the staff must check everything, so you have to undergo a chest Xray and blood tests to see if your troponin level is high. The blood doesn't usually contain troponin, so if it is present, it indicates if you have recently had a heart attack, or one is taking place at that moment. The more protein that is released, the greater the damage is done to the heart muscle.

Then, of course, when it proves to be a panic attack you feel embarrassed, but still must pay the bill! However, I would say to you that it is worth going to the emergency room if you think you are having a heart attack. It can feel exactly the same as a panic attack, and a visit might save your life.

What is the difference between a panic attack and an anxiety attack?

Sometimes it is difficult to tell a panic attack and an anxiety attack apart, but there is a subtle difference. When you are very worried, anxiety can build up over a long period of time until you are overwhelmed. This is an anxiety attack because it takes longer to reach critical mass than a panic attack which is sudden and comes out of nowhere, even when you are not feeling anxious.

What is panic disorder?

Panic disorder is diagnosed when you have repeated

panic attacks lasting several minutes. This needs treatment with medication as it is very disabling and causes a great deal of distress. Be sure to contact your doctor if you are suffering a lot of panic attacks.

How to stop a panic attack

If you are having a panic attack, follow these steps:

- Ground yourself by leaning against a wall, or sit down
- Feel the ground beneath your feet
- Take three deep breaths (if possible)
- Focus on one thing in the room
- Keep your focus on that object
- Breathe deeply
- Notice its shape
- Notice its color
- Notice any other details about it
- Keep your focus on the object for two minutes
- Breathe into it
- Let the panic wash over you and subside

Hopefully, this will alleviate the frightening symptoms of a panic attack.

Chapter 14
Anger and rage

Anger seems to be a sore subject when it comes to bipolar 1. Many people say it is not a symptom of bipolar 1 at all, yet nearly everyone I speak to, says they have a problem with anger on occasion.

Many also have a problem with rage. That is when things get really out of hand, and it is often too late to gain control. Violent rage can be another problem with bipolar, but violence never solved any problem, it only makes things worse. Alcohol in large quantities can also cause an angry response.

Many women have an anger problem associated with menstruation, too, and extra care should be taken to stay calm at this time of the month. Get more sleep than usual and relax during the daytime if you can.

It seems to me that anger is part of bipolar 1, and you should do everything you can to mitigate it. I have found that doctors are not sympathetic when it comes to this side of bipolar, and some do not recognize it at all. They are quite willing to say that irritability is a symptom of bipolar 1, but they won't go as far as to say that anger and rage are symptoms at all.

Some people who take Lithium report irritability and anger as a side effect, and it is true that it can take a while to get used to the chemicals or elements in your body. The best thing is to wait for your body to adjust to the medication before seeing the doctor. Never stop or change doses without medical advice. That goes for all medications. They all need to be given under strict supervision from a doctor.

How does anger affect your life?

The problem I had with anger is it gravely affected my relationships with family and friends and caused me a lot of problems at work. Many of my jobs have been lost to bipolar anger, and I always regret losing my temper afterwards when it is too late.

Irritability is one thing, but when you are angry you say and do things you usually regret later. Most people don't want to be around you when you are angry, and who can blame them?

Irritability and anger are very draining. Anger is real. And it is exhausting. When you are tired already, it is much easier to get angry than when you are well rested. So, I'll stress again how sleep is very important in bipolar. It certainly helps with anger.

Of course, anger is a healthy emotion if expressed properly. It is good to get your problems out in the open and not bottle them up inside. Anger seems to be one of the emotions that are treated negatively, and a lot of people have a hard time expressing it in a healthy way. When anger is suppressed to boiling point, that is when you snap, and the fall out can be horrendous. It can even send you to jail.

Many families have emotions that are safe to express and emotions that are taboo. One of those taboo emotions is often anger. This is a problem when you grow up because you have stuffed your anger for so many years that if something major goes wrong you erupt.

Are mood swings affected by anger?

People get angry during mania, but they also get angry when they are depressed. You can understand the anger in mania to a certain extent as everything is speeded up and your thoughts are coming fast. It is sometimes difficult to tolerate how other people seem to be functioning so slowly, but losing your temper won't help the situation, either. Unfortunately, a lot of people are not in control when they are manic, and they must suffer the consequences of their anger afterwards.

Anger in depression is a bit harder to understand, but when you think how irritable you can get when depressed, it makes sense. Being depressed is depressing! Yes. That is exactly what it is. Being in a negative frame of mind and thinking negative thoughts can easily cause a bout of anger.

Other people can simply annoy you because they don't understand depression and make unreasonable demands on you. Of course, to them, these demands seem quite reasonable, they may not understand why you can't get up and do things, for example, but you know that is not possible half the time. If things like this should occur, it is very easy to get angry, which of course alienates people and gets you nowhere.

Does anger affect the body?

Anger is very hard on the body. When you are angry, you are more prone to high blood pressure and heart attacks. The fight or flight mechanism comes into play, and the hormones adrenaline and cortisol are swirling around in the body.

It is also said that a hostile person has hardening of the arteries and heart disease at a young age. Therefore, it is so important to get your anger under control. Let alone all the broken relationships anger can leave you with.

How do you control your anger?

But how do you control all this anger? How do you calm yourself down when you are out of control? Of course, the answer is not to allow yourself to get into such an extreme state in the first place, but this is much easier said than done. We all have a lot of stress in our lives these days, let alone when we are unwell with bipolar 1 mood swings.

Fortunately, there are things you can do to help yourself, but some things are more difficult than others. One thing which I find helpful is letting off steam by moving the body, maybe by going to the gym, going for a fast walk, or dancing around the room to loud music. All these things calm me down. You might try them, or they might not be right for you. It is all trial and error when it comes to bipolar 1.

I also find writing things down tremendously helpful and write pages of notes when I am angry. I keep a journal and record what is happening in my life every day. I make a note of what I am doing, and how I am feeling, and if I see things are building up to a crescendo I go for a long walk.

You need to do everything you can to prevent stress from building up in the body. It might be a good idea to initiate a relaxation routine. Doing relaxation techniques can be very helpful to calm the body down. You will need to do them on a regular basis when you are calm. Be consistent. Consistency is key when it comes to anger management.

I shall talk more about relaxation techniques in a later chapter.

How can other people help?

Therapy can be helpful for anger issues as well. It is a safe place to discuss the difficulties you are having with control. Talking to somebody when calm can help you see what steps can be taken to handle the problems in your life without getting angry. It is always better to plan ahead, if at all possible.

Talk therapy is particularly helpful for working on anger issues as it really helps to share the problem with another person. Many therapists do anger management training which can be helpful as well.

A good support system is always a great thing, too, as you can share your feelings with people who care about your wellbeing. But I am only too aware that not everybody has a good support system, and many people have no support system at all.

Triggers are very important when it comes to anger issues. Don't forget to write out all the things that make you angry when you are well so that you can avoid them when you are in an irritable mood.

The important thing is to forgive yourself for your anger. If you didn't have this illness, you wouldn't have all this anger, would you? Be kind to yourself. So many people suffer from low self-esteem and losing control can have a major negative effect on how you feel about yourself.

What is rage like?

Rage is another thing entirely. If you have ever had a rage episode you will know what I am talking about. It is beyond awful and consumes you like nothing else. I cannot tell you how exhausting rage is, and how harmful it is to the body.

I went through a few months of rage once and was a nervous wreck. The rage began the moment I woke up and went on until I went to bed. It was very distressing. It is difficult to imagine a woman in her 70s stomping around the house, swearing, and almost resorting to violence. The most I did was thump my computer, but my wrist suffered for many weeks after that. Oh, the phone got some very harsh treatment as well, and often went flying across the room when I was in a rage. Luckily, phones don't easily break. They must be made with bipolar 1 rage in mind.

I went to anger management and sat through six weeks of exercises to gain control of my mood. Unfortunately, it was useless for me at that time. It didn't do a thing for my rage. Eventually, I got my doctor to prescribe a medication that helped to a large extent. Medicine routines are pre-scribed on an individual basis, so it is no use suggesting you use the same thing. You will need to discuss medica-tions with your doctor if you are suffering from bipolar 1 rage.

I have no idea what I was raging about. That was prob-ably the worst of all. I was simply out of control the whole time and suffered a great deal. I am always calm these days because I do an exercise routine three times a week at the gym and keep up a relaxation program at home. I make sure I get a lot of sleep and take naps in the middle of the day if I am tired. Finally, I can say I am rage-free and happy.

Family and friends

If you love someone who has an anger problem, you will know how it tries your patience. If it is really bad, it may be frightening, too. Who knows what will happen next when you are in the same room as a person in an angry mood, let alone someone in a rage? Nasty things get said and things can go flying around the room.

The best thing I know of is to get out of their way. There is no sense trying to reason with a person in bipolar 1 rage. And it is no good asking them to take deep breaths and count to ten. I have not found this technique helpful at all. In fact, it is downright annoying, and can make a person even more angry when the suggestion comes up.

Going from 0 to 10 in bipolar 1 rage can be very rapid and scary to watch. I think the more you try to calm someone down the worse things can get.

Always remember that the person is not necessarily mad with you, so do not take it personally. If you can sit down with them when they are well and talk about what to do when they are angry, it might be helpful.

If you are lucky, you might be able to get them to come up with a plan to prevent any damage and sign it. Then you can show it to them when they start to get angry. Don't leave it too long, though, as this can annoy a person even more.

At any rate, encourage the person to never miss their medication and go to see the doctor before things get out of control.

Chapter 15
Feeling overwhelmed

There is no doubt about it, bipolar disorder can be overwhelming to cope with every day, and you never get a day off. Other people may get a temporary sickness and have to cope with that for a few days or a few weeks, then they are fine and back to normal again. But when you have bipolar 1, it doesn't take a vacation. It is always there, and always needs to be dealt with in the best way possible. This can feel overwhelming.

I have always found bipolar disorder to be a full-time job that needs special coping skills every day. I used not to think like that and got myself into all kinds of trouble. I used to stay out late, drinking at parties when I was in my twenties, but paid the price with mood swings all too often.

Now, I realize that bipolar 1 needs work. We shall discuss that in more detail in Part Six.

Bipolar 1 is overwhelming

You will probably agree that living with bipolar 1 can be overwhelming. This applies mostly when you are having a manic episode as you tend to have racing thoughts where your thoughts come flooding in at a rapid rate and you can't keep up with them. Racing thoughts come with the territory when you have mania, and they are very hard to deal with.

I used to get racing thoughts quite often with mania, but since I have been well, they have ceased. The way I dealt with them when they did appear was to try to relax. I used to lie on the couch for a while, and just let the thoughts come and go. I did not judge them, or even pay them close attention, I just watched them coming and going. After a while, they ceased, and I was free until the next manic episode.

People with bipolar 1 are hyper-sensitive. Everything affects you, every thought or feeling seems way more important than it really is. And you can get easily hurt when people treat you badly. You take it to heart and upset yourself for hours or days. It is hard to manage your daily life when you feel hurt and upset. There are just too many demands being made of you.

The best way to deal with these thoughts is to learn not to let them bother you, but that is a lesson for another day!

Being overwhelmed when you are depressed can add to your feelings of guilt quite easily. But when you are depressed, you will realize that you are totally unable to keep up with life and all its demands, so you will have to deal with them later when you feel well again.

It is easy to think you are the only one in the world suffering from stress, but of course this is not so as everybody has a lot of stress in their lives these days. That is the era we live in.

It is good to deal with stress with relaxation exercises, and we shall talk about that more later.

Bipolar 1 is exhausting

Just trying to keep up with the program of living is exhausting, yet it must be done every day, or you will get sick. It is tempting to go to bed late, for example, but you will soon regret it. If you do this too often, a manic mood swing is very likely to follow. Once again, it is very important to be aware of how sleep is imperative to your wellbeing in bipolar disorder.

Missing meals, or eating junk food, is another no-no when you have bipolar 1. It is annoying to have to avoid the things you love, but if it can keep your mood-free it is better.

Today's technology can be overwhelming

Personally, I find it difficult to live in today's technological world. Many of you who read this will be a lot younger than me and have learned how to use computers and other devices in school. But when you are in your seventies, life can go whizzing by too fast, and it is difficult to keep up.

Just making a phone call these days can be hazardous to people with bipolar 1 as you can hardly ever get a real live person on the line. All you get are menus, and sometimes I find I have a hard time keeping up with which button to press because the automated voice speaks too fast. Then I often push the wrong button and end up having to start all over again!

I often wonder how people who are really old – older than me – manage in today's world if they have bipolar 1. I don't envy them. Bipolar 1 can definitely affect your cognition with age which makes it doubly difficult to contend with life.

Ways of coping with the feelings of being overwhelmed

I heard of somebody who collects little quotes and mantras and puts them on their calendar. Then when the day comes, they will get little words of encouragement, saying things like, *"You are doing extremely well,"* or, *"Today is another wonderful day."* You could do this yourself or put quotes in your journal or make a separate board for quotes on Pinterest. Pleasing, positive photographs also make good support for you when you are overwhelmed.

You might have heard of a Vision Board, or you might even have done one yourself. If you want to try one out, it is easy, and many people say the things you plan for your future come to fruition, especially if you can see them in front of you every day.

Vision Board

Take a board of some sort about three feet square. You can buy foam boards at Dollar Tree if you like – that is a very inexpensive way to begin. Then look for pictures of things you would like to have in your future. You can put pictures of a man or woman who looks like the kind of person you might like to marry, cars, houses, holidays, or all kinds of things you think of as unattainable right now. You might have your own pictures already, or you can find hundreds of them in magazines or online.

Find pictures that suggest what you would like in your future but find it difficult to attain. Now arrange them on your board like a collage and hang it where you can see it. You will be able to add things to your board at any time. Good luck with this and I hope your future dreams come true.

If you don't have any magazines, you could probably find lots of them at a second-hand store.

Pace yourself

Another thing to do is to pace yourself. Not everything needs to be done at breakneck speed. If you slow down and take it easy you will likely find that you are better able to deal with things.

I have a bad habit of walking too fast, for no particular reason. I often find myself totally out of breath just by walking to the supermarket from the car park, or even when taking a walk in the park. Why I don't walk slowly is hard to fathom. I sometimes see my reflection in the glass walls of the post office, and marvel at the way I am walking. Now, I have to force myself to slow down, and I find I can if I try.

Don't make promises you can't keep. Sometimes, it is tempting to take on too much without realizing it, and people have a habit of forcing more and more things on you, if you are not careful. Learn how to say, "No."

At work, you may be too willing to take on more projects, but when you have bipolar 1 it is important to know your limits to avoid getting overwhelmed.

Pets are great for slowing you down. Take a nice walk round the block with your dog, play with your cat. Pets can take any amount of attention; they never get fed up with it. Playing with pets is also calming, and if you do it regularly, you can avoid mood swings from building up.

I can recommend therapy when it comes to avoiding feelings of being overwhelmed. My therapist has taught me a lot about pacing myself and keeping calm. And it is nice to have someone to talk to as well. This is where a good support system is great when it comes to bipolar 1.

I shall discuss other ways of dealing with your daily life in Parts Four and Five, but for now we should agree that we do need to take care of ourselves in order to stop that horrible feeling of being overwhelmed.

Overwhelmed with everyday life

What we have been discussing is about living with bipolar 1 which can be overwhelming if you don't work on it daily, but there is another form of being overwhelmed which may well cause you a lot of problems day to day.

I used to get overwhelmed when I had too much to do. It was usually my fault because I had let things pile up by procrastinating over them. Then, for whatever reason, they all needed attention at the same time, and I totally lost it. It was awful. I used to stare at all the paperwork on my table and not know where to start. I would come out in a sweat and think I was going to faint.

That is what I call being overwhelmed.

I no longer get overwhelmed like that because I do my best to tackle things before deadlines appear. It is a discipline that is well worth practicing. Now I apply time management techniques to solve the problem.

Time management

1) Get a trash can, sticky notes, and a pen.

2) Pile up all the papers on the table.

3) Go through the pile slowly and, with your sticky notes, label all the pieces of paper **CALL**, **WRITE**, **SORT OUT** or **FILE**.

4) When you come to spam, toss it in the trash.

5) Now that you have your big pile in order, go through it again and put all the papers from **CALL**, **WRITE**, **SORT OUT** and **FILE** together. Make four neat piles.

When your four piles are in order, you can either tackle them there and then, or leave them on the table for another day because being overwhelmed takes up all your energy.

That is what I do now which prevents that awful feeling of being overwhelmed before it starts. I leave the neat piles that day, then when I feel better, I go back to them and sort them out. Try it. You might be pleasantly surprised.

Clutter

Clutter also makes me feel overwhelmed. If I was trying to find something to wear and my closet was full to bursting, I used to get in a panic and feel overwhelmed.

The best way to cure this problem is to toss out things you haven't worn for a year and keep your closet tidy. I am a bit OCD, so my closet is all in color-coded order now. But at least I can find things.

I once had a business called Sort it Out, and I used to sort out people's closets, cupboards, garages, kitchens, toy rooms, offices or any other place that needed sorting. I even sorted out a fishpond once. That was my favorite job. I first took out all the plants and repotted the ones that were too big for their pots. Then I took out all the fish and cleaned the water. Lastly, I put everything back in again. Phew! I was exhausted, but it was fun.

If you have a lot of clutter to sort out, here is a tried-and-true technique I always used for dealing with it:

Clutter buster

1) Find three very large boxes or plastic bags.

2) Label them: ***TRASH***, ***TREASURE***, ***DONATE***.

3) Get an alarm clock and set it for 15 minutes.

4) Go through any closet or cupboard in the house by taking everything out first.

5) As you take things out of the closet or cupboard, put them in the ***TRASH*** if you are not going to use them again, put them back into the closet or cupboard if they are ***TREASURES*** and you are determined to keep them, or put them in the ***DONATE*** bag or box if you think somebody else could use them.

The most important thing is you only do this in spurts of 15 minutes at a time as it is a very emotional exercise and can cause a lot of stress if you try to do too much at once. You can always go back to it another day or put the alarm on for another 15 minutes after you have had a coffee break.

Be sure not to put everything back in the closet or cup–board! If it is **TRASH** take it out of the house immediately, and if it is **DONATE** take it out to the car. That way you won't be tempted to put it all back again.

Also, if you find things like photo albums that have been sitting there for ages waiting to be sorted, put them to one side and get on with the task in hand. Photo albums are for another day.

You can then stand back and admire your handiwork. Reward yourself with a bowl of ice cream.

Appointments

Another thing I find overwhelming is having too many appointments or errands to run in one day. Now I make sure that I don't tackle more than three things in one day, and life is much less stressful.

Chapter 16
Bipolar blips!

I have been ill with bipolar 1 since the age of fifteen, so have had ample opportunity to study how I react to things. Over the years, I have noticed that I do have euthymic periods where I am free of bipolar 1 mania and depression, but these episodes are not completely free of bipolar symptoms.

You may have noticed this yourself and wondered what was happening. I have never got an answer to this problem from the medical community. I have had a hard time in between episodes because my symptoms were alienating other people.

It is difficult to describe what I mean as it is hard to observe yourself and come to a clear conclusion, but I must tell you that I had what I call bipolar blips more or less all the time.

Looking back, I can say that not only was I stupid, I felt stupid all the time. I am a fairly intelligent person but found myself saying and doing the weirdest things in between episodes of mania and depression.

Once, in church, a young couple announced that half their house had burned down, and they needed a place to stay. Normally, if I had been well, I would not have done anything about that because, although I live on my own, I use my spare bedroom as a studio when I want to paint.

However, on this one occasion, I rushed forward, tears streaming down my face, and suggested this young couple come and stay with me although I only have one bed. I figured that they could use my bed while I slept on the couch. I never considered the fact that I would become very uncomfortable on my couch and would soon regret offering them my bed. Luckily, they turned me down because somebody else, with more room than me, offered to have them in their house. But as you can see, I had a bipolar 1 blip!

Another time, also in church, we had to do something for a talent contest. Of course, I could have sat it out, and would have done so if I was sensible, but instead I read out a piece of the novel I was writing to the congregation instead. I am not a good reader and soon enough I was stumbling over my own words. I found myself thumping my papers with my fist like someone possessed in front of everybody.

Would I have done that if I was well? I hardly think so. It was just another bipolar blip.

Another time, I stood up and announced that I had bipolar disorder and had many ups and downs that were called highs and lows. It was none of the congregation's business, of course, and that blip cost me a lot of so-called friends because people shunned me after that.

These are some of my examples, all in church as it happens, but I am sure you have said and done stupid things in your life, too. When you look back, your toes curl up in your shoes. But things have been said and done, and you have had bipolar 1 blips.

The cause of blips

I am sorry to say I do not know the cause of all these blips. I have mentioned them to a couple of doctors in the past, but nobody has given me a satisfactory explanation. I imagine that the brain chemicals are really unbalanced when this happens, but that has never been confirmed.

In fact, I have found that doctors do not recognize these blips at all and like to divide the bipolar 1 experience into purely manic and depressive episodes. But if you are like me, you will know that is not true.

I do know that I have never lived down these blips. Even now, I cringe when I think of all the stupid things I have said and done in public. I now spend most of my time alone, and am feeling very well lately, so I am not concerned with what other people think of me.

Chapter 17
Aging

This subject concerns me because I am no longer a young person with bipolar 1, but it may not concern you just yet. Maybe by the time you reach your fifties or sixties, they will have come up with something to ease the symptoms of bipolar 1.

For those that are over fifty, I do hope this will be helpful to you.

Studies on aging

At the present time, the effects of aging in people with bipolar 1 has not been studied sufficiently, in my view, so they have not come up with any definitive answers. When I tried to research this, I found that various studies contradicted one another, so it is difficult to say one way or another what aging does to a person with bipolar 1.

The thing the studies had in common is you tend to age more rapidly when you have bipolar disorder. In fact, you can expect to live nine to twenty years less than the general population, but that is often due to the fact that some have bipolar with a dual diagnosis. This means they self-medicate with various substances which can shorten their life span. Also, there is a greater risk of suicide when you have bipolar1.

Interestingly enough, it seems that if you took Lithium, you are likely to live longer than those who didn't. Also, if you have paid attention to diet and avoided obesity and smoking you will likely live a longer life with bipolar 1. This, of course, is not true for everyone.

Aging and comorbidities in bipolar 1 disorder

When you are older (over the age of fifty) you tend to have three to four physical comorbidities to contend with as well as bipolar disorder; cardiovascular disease, diabetes, and hypertension being the most common.

Also, people over the age of fifty are four times more likely to be hospitalized. I fall into that category as I have hypothyroidism, high blood pressure and autonomic neuropathy to contend with. This means taking many more medications in one day along with my bipolar medications. And, indeed, I have spent a lot of time in the hospital.

Effects of aging on bipolar 1 disorder moods

With regard to mood swings, when you are older you have less mania than when you were younger but can suffer more episodes of depression. Fortunately, you are less likely to suffer episodes of psychosis.

You are better able to cope with mood swings later in life because you will have accepted that you have a mental illness and have better coping skills. You will also know your triggers and tend to avoid them more than when you were younger.

Also, when you are in your fifties, your family will more than likely have left home so, hopefully, your stress level will have lowered. (I could be wrong in that!)

Conversely, when you are older, you can have more hospital stays with depression mainly because your support system is likely to shrink due to the death of your friends and relatives. You may also be alone more often with time on your hands.

All these symptoms are exacerbated if you did not receive treatment at the beginning of your illness. There is no doubt that, if you get treatment early for bipolar 1, you will be healthier than otherwise.

Hobbies and interests

It is very hard to generalize about people's lives whether they are old or young. People are different and have different circumstances. But when it comes to older people, it is a good idea to have hobbies and interests, and even do volunteer work that will keep you busy in the community.

You may be worried about memory problems related to bipolar 1 medication. That is why it is important to keep your brain active with brain teasers in later years.

The internet is also a great boon for when you are elderly, you can keep in touch with family and friends through social media and learn things that you may not have had access to before. You can also do puzzles and play card games online. I have a lot of fun with this myself.

If you are still able to work in a stress-free environment, you will likely do well because you have a ready-made social life and feel you are being useful. This has a positive effect on the aging process.

You are also likely to do better in therapy as you are usually recognized for your age and experience. My therapist says he sees people who are over fifty most of time because that is the time of life when they are serious about sorting out their problems.

If you live alone, you are likely to have special challenges because you will have more time to think and ruminate over the shame and guilt of past indiscretions.

You may not have any friends or family left, and therefore lack support when you are sick. Older people with bipolar 1 can be very lonely, and they can become depressed through lack of association with the outside world.

There are often financial problems that come with aging and bipolar 1. Many people are overqualified and work at menial jobs, and many others are unable to work at all. If you are able to do part time work, that can be a real bonus when you are a senior. It will get you out of the house, so you can avoid depression.

Chapter 18
Menopause

I was in France when I started getting strange physical symptoms, but even though I was a nurse, it never occurred to me that I might be starting menopause. I was forty-seven. Surely, things like that were for old people? Or so I thought at the time.

The symptoms of my bipolar 1 disorder began to reappear, as well, but I still didn't attribute them to menopause.

My husband and I came back from France and went to Miami where we bought an RV to tour the country, and by this time I was quite sick with bipolar 1. I went to a strange doctor in Miami and complained about all my symptoms, and he said, *"Lady, you are forty-seven. You are in menopause."* That was my entry into this strange new world. I went in kicking and screaming!

If you are fortunate and your marriage/partnership has survived thus far, beware. Rocky times are ahead. Men suffer from menopause, as well, I am told. They even suffer from our symptoms.

The symptoms of menopause

The symptoms of menopause are many and varied. Here are a few of them:

Systemic	weight gain, heavy night sweats
Heart	palpitations
Breasts	enlargement/pain
Skin	hot flashes, dry, itchy, tingling
Joints	sore, stiff, backpain
Urinary	incontinence, urgency
Psychological	dizziness, interrupted sleep, poor memory, irritability, sad, tired, confused, loss of libido, brain fog, crying spells
Transitional	shorter or longer periods bleeding between periods
Vagina	dry, pain on intercourse

There are other illnesses such as hypertension, thyroid disease, diabetes, and calcium or vitamin deficiency that could be to blame for these symptoms, so it is always best to see your doctor as soon as the symptoms start.

Menopause and bipolar disorder

As you can see, you have a lot to contend with during menopause, and if you add bipolar 1 to the mix, you will find that life can be really hard indeed. You will also find that it is difficult to differentiate the physical symptoms from the psychological ones. If your bipolar 1 symptoms get worse, you will need to get a medication change.

I had my worst times during menopause, and no amount of medication changes helped me at all. I kept losing my temper and having rage episodes, and slept a great deal of the time, too. My hot flashes were particularly bad, and I counted twenty-five a day, on average. I had to stick my head in the freezer for relief!

Menopause goes on for much longer than you think, and you can have hot flashes or night sweats for many years afterwards. The symptoms may go away, only to return when you least expect it. I sometimes get hot flashes even now, after more than twenty years.

Support in menopause

You are going to need a lot of support from any family and friends that have survived your bipolar 1 disorder. Also, try peer support for help. You will need to enlist the help of your doctor and therapist, as well. You may also want to make friends with your pharmacist. I found the most relief came from compounded medications, so you might like to try them for yourself if your doctor advises you.

Your children have usually left home by this time, and you may be alone with your partner. If you can divide the household chores, then you will be better able to cope. Nobody has any idea what you are feeling like, so you need to be your own best friend. Take it easy if you can. Rest in menopause is essential.

Hormone replacement therapy

You will need to speak to your doctor about HRT if you decide to go that route. HRT adds the hormone estrogen which is lacking in menopause.

Here are a few things you can do to help yourself during menopause:

- Write notes of encouragement to yourself
- Keep a journal
- Take naps
- Listen to calming music
- Work on your goals
- Buy yourself flowers
- Stock up on ice cream

It is well to note that some people have a much easier time in menopause, so you may be one of the lucky ones.

Be sure to keep all your psychiatric appointments, too, as you may need your medication adjusted at this time. Also, try therapy, if you haven't done so already. Therapy can be very helpful for older people.

Chapter 19
Substance abuse

As I mentioned before, people with bipolar 1 often have three to four comorbidities to live with. Some physical ones are:

- Thyroid disease
- Hypertension
- Heart disease
- Kidney disease
- Liver disease
- Diabetes

When you have bipolar 1, and are also physically ill, it can be very difficult. Because of this, and for many other reasons, some people self-medicate in order to cope with the symptoms. This is where problems can arise.

Dual-diagnosis

Many people with bipolar 1 disorder have a comorbidity of harmful substance abuse. It is very difficult to treat both conditions concurrently.

It is thought that 50 to 60% of people with bipolar 1 disorder will also have a problem with alcohol or drugs at some point in their illness. Some studies suggest that it is more like 75%.

The reasons for dual-diagnoses is not completely understood, but it is thought that it is one of three things:

- Genetics
- Pleasure-seeking
- Self-medicating

If you have an addictive personality, you may have a problem with alcohol, over the counter medications, prescription drugs, nicotine, or illegal substances.

The problem is, even though you know a habit will harm you, if you are addicted to it, you will continue to do it. As everybody knows, if you touch a hot stove, you usually learn that you should not touch it again, but with chemical addiction this does not always follow. You touch it with the other hand to see if it hurts.

If you have a dual-diagnosis it is considered a serious psychiatric disorder. You may use substances to self-medicate imagining this will help your bipolar 1 symptoms, but as bipolar is a mood disorder, substances can worsen your mood and make you feel very sick.

If you use alcohol and sedatives to help you sleep when you are in a manic episode, you will be deprived of the necessary REM sleep which will eventually cause difficulty in falling asleep.

Similarly, if you do cocaine and amphetamines to relieve the symptoms of a depressive episode, you can cause a great deal of harm as the brain becomes depleted of necessary neurotransmitters. It can also cause psychosis, paranoia, or even suicide.

Having a dual-diagnosis can cause a loss of important relationships, loss of jobs, and legal problems like DUI. Unfortunately, you may end up in jail where you are unlikely to get the correct treatment.

Treatment for dual-diagnosis

Ideally, bipolar disorder and substance abuse should be treated concurrently, but this is not always possible. Sometimes you cannot afford to treat both of your conditions at the same time, or the facilities are just not available.

In order to get the best treatment, you should get help with medications for bipolar disorder from a psychiatrist, and treatment for substance abuse from an abuse counselor.

Treatment for dual-diagnosis is as follows:

- Rehabilitation centers that offer centralized care on a one-to-one basis from a licensed professional.

- Medication for an underlying bipolar 1 disorder.

- Psychotherapy to manage the everyday complications of using bipolar medications and drugs – the aim of this is to reduce the use of substances. Various methods can be used such as cognitive behavioral therapy (CBT), or dialectical behavioral therapy (DBT).

- Group support, either through a peer group at a clinic, or alcoholics anonymous (AA), or narcotics anonymous (NA).

Unfortunately, you may not respond to conventional treatment for dual-diagnosis, then you will not get the care you need. This can be caused by several factors, but usually has to do with bipolar moods:

- Absence of motivation during a depressive episode

- Being unfocused during a manic episode

The best thing you can do is to advocate for yourself to get the help you need. If this is not possible, hopefully, you will have a good support system where someone else can advocate for you. If you are still not happy, never be afraid to get a second opinion.

Chapter 20
Suicide

If you have bipolar 1 disorder, you are at a much greater risk of committing suicide than members of the general public – both suicide attempts and completing the act. In fact, 4–19% of people with bipolar in the US, and in the rest of the world, do actually commit suicide, and 20 – 60% make at least one attempt. Many people make repeated attempts until they succeed.

People who are untreated with medication for bipolar disorder, are far more likely to complete the act than those who are in a treatment program.

Also, as I explained before, people coming out of a depressive episode are more likely to commit suicide because they have the impetus when they are well.

There are many risk factors involved:

- Early onset of the illness
- Substance abuse
- Family history of substance abuse
- Previous attempted suicides
- Family history of sexual or physical abuse
- Family or friends who committed suicide

- Unemployment and loss of financial stability
- Keeping firearms, knives, and prescription medications in the house
- Newly discharged from psychiatric hospital

As previously mentioned, if you take Lithium there is a much greater chance that you will not commit suicide. In fact, many studies show that people who take Lithium are less likely to have suicidal ideation (thoughts of committing suicide.)

When you have mania and depression as part of bipolar 1, you will find that caregivers will often give you more attention when you are manic than when you are depressed. And, unfortunately, it is usually during depression that you are more susceptible to feeling suicidal.

Many caregivers are more vigilant when it comes to mania. They tend to leave depressive episodes up to the doctor to cope with, but psychiatrists have been known to withhold anti-depressant medication when people are depressed because they do not want to run the risk of a manic reaction.

After a particularly destructive manic episode comes deep depression for many people. If you do mood charts you will notice a sharp drop shortly after the manic episode ends.

The guilt and shame that often accompanies depression becomes far greater after an episode of mania, particular one where you lost complete control and caused damage to your social life. Sometimes, after you have upset family and friends, they will not forgive you, so you are left alone to cope with your depression.

It is quite common to be completely abandoned during a depressive episode. This is unfortunate, but it does happen.

This abandonment can lead to a lack of the will to live, a feeling of not being cared for, and missed psychiatric appointments when they are needed the most. Many people are just too sick to get out of bed.

Here are some warning signs that you are at risk of a suicide attempt:

- Talking about suicide
- Talking about death in general
- Commenting that you are feeling worthless, hopeless, or helpless
- Feeling that it would be better if you were out of the way
- Worsening depression
- Putting your affairs in order
- Insomnia
- Restlessness and agitation

If you feel suicidal, or are just thinking about death in general, do reach out to the:

The National Suicide Prevention Hotline: 1 800-273-8255

Here we have discussed suicide in detail, so you should feel more prepared to cope with it. If you should recognize any of these symptoms in yourself, it is imperative that you seek help from somebody immediately, preferably the mental health professionals.

It is quite normal to think of death and wanting to die when you are depressed as it is a common symptom, but when you begin to make plans for your death, that is the time you need help. Don't wait until it is too late, reach out to your doctor, your family, your peer support group, or the National Suicide Prevention Hotline.

As they say,
   "suicide is a permanent solution to a temporary problem."

Summing it up

We have covered a few complex topics in Part Three. As a result, you will know more about how you can treat your bipolar 1 disorder. Some of these things may not apply to you, but may be of use to another person. Here are the things we have discussed:

- Anxiety and panic attacks
- Anger and rage
- Feeling overwhelmed
- Bipolar blips
- Aging
- Menopause
- Substance abuse
- Suicide

Family and friends

If you are a support person for somebody with bipolar 1, be aware that people do in fact often talk about their intentions to commit suicide before they act. When this happens, it is tempting to ignore it, say they are looking for attention, or to laugh it off. But you should pay attention as it could save their life.

Should you be faced with this situation, and your loved one is feeling suicidal, be sure to put things like extra medications, knives, or guns out of their reach. These things are very tempting when a person is desperate, and if they are sincere about committing suicide, they won't hesitate to use them.

Many a family have borne guilt for years because they didn't listen when their loved one was crying out for help. Do not be fooled. This is serious. Bipolar 1 is a deadly disease.

If your family member or friend is sincere about committing suicide, and they have made a plan, make sure that someone stays with them, then call 911. They may not be happy about going to the hospital, but it is the only place where they will be safe. There they will get 24/7 care which they will likely be unable to get at home.

PART FOUR
TREATMENT FOR BIPOLAR 1 DISORDER

Chapter 21
Psychiatrists

The standard treatment for bipolar 1 disorder is medication and therapy in one form or another. Medication aims to control the mood swings and therapy helps you cope with everyday life.

If you don't have a reliable doctor at the moment, you will need to find one to supply you with the correct medications. You can go to any doctor and get a prescription for bipolar medications, but it is usually better to see a psychiatrist as these doctors have had extra training in psychiatry and are better able to treat your illness. Also, if you have a crisis, you are more likely to get the help you need.

Your psychiatrist should be there to help you cope with your mental illness. It is no use giving a person a diagnosis and a prescription without helping them understand what is wrong with them. Your doctor should be your confidant. You will need a confidant as time passes because many problems will emerge in your life when you have bipolar 1. Your doctor should also be able to help you understand the symptoms of the illness as well as explaining the different medications and their side effects.

Unfortunately, you get a very limited time with a psychiatrist these days. Some visits are as short as ten to fifteen minutes. So, if this is the case with you, be sure to organize this appointment so that you get all your questions answered before leaving the doctor's office. It is no use thinking of something when your visit is over.

If you want to be sure that your questions are answered properly, do write them down before you go to see the psychiatrist. Then make sure you write down all the answers he gives you so that you can go over them when you get home. It is amazing how easy it is to forget what the doctor has said, then it would have been a wasted visit.

Going to see a psychiatrist can be a very daunting experience for some people because they know they will have to share unpleasant symptoms with them, but doctors will be attuned to this, as they are used to seeing people with all kinds of mental problems.

What do you do if you don't have a good relationship with your psychiatrist?

If you don't feel at ease with your psychiatrist, it is a good idea to find a different one who will be interested in getting to know you and helping you cope with your diagnosis. Of course, not everybody has the opportunity to change practitioners, so you will need to be as clear about your needs as possible. This is where it is important to advocate for yourself.

If you are unable to find a psychiatrist in your area

If you are unable to find a psychiatrist, you might try going to NAMI (National Alliance for Mental Illness) online. They will be able to find someone in your area to help you.

You can also try the National Association of Free and Charitable Clinics. Some teaching and academic institutions also offer various forms of psychiatry and therapy, and you can often find help from religious groups. If you are a Veteran, you may find help within that organization.

Insurance

When you see a new doctor, one of the first things you will want to be aware of is your eligibility for treatment. If you have a good insurance policy that includes psychiatric care, you are fortunate, as mental health can be excluded by some companies. Do call the company first and make sure you are eligible for mental health treatment, then you can see what your plan covers. Also, ask if you will need a doctor's referral or not. It is always best to go in with your eyes open so that you don't get caught off guard with unexpected charges.

For the uninsured

If you don't have insurance, you may need to seek help in the community. Your doctor may know the name of a clinic in your area. It is sometimes difficult to get help with mental health problems, but you will need help if you are going to get well and stay well.

Psychiatric medications tend to be expensive, so if you cannot afford a medication that is recommended by your psychiatrist, it is best to discuss using a generic instead of a brand name. Sometimes, however, the brand name medication is the only one that is suitable for you. Don't despair, many medications can be bought from the manufacturer for a discount price. Also, several manufacturers have Patient Assistance Programs which make medications affordable, or even free of charge. Just write or phone the company and ask them to send you a form to fill in.

One of my medications is very expensive indeed, so I am glad that I can get it through their Patient Assistance Program. If you are unable to get help this way, ask your doctor for some samples.

Chapter 22
Medication

゜ᑕ❀ᗡ゜

Treatment of bipolar 1 has come a long way in the past several years due to extensive research and a plethora of new drugs that have come onto the market. At one time, a doctor would prescribe time-tested drugs because he knew they would work, but several had serious side effects. Now, with the introduction of new medications, doctors are prescribing them more and more because they are seeing better results in their patients with fewer serious side effects.

New medications

When you get a new medication prescribed by your doctor, make sure you read the literature that is provided by the pharmacy. Check to see if you have been given the right medication and the right dosage. I have found mistakes a couple of times and have had to go back to the pharmacy. Medicine colors and shapes change, too, according to the manufacturer the pharmacist uses, so be sure to give them a call to clarify.

Also check to see if your medication can be taken with ones you are already taking, and if in doubt call the psychiatrist or the pharmacist. More than likely the doctor has already checked this, but it is better to be safe than sorry. It could save your life.

Side effects

Be sure to monitor side effects. Every medication has side effects, even aspirin. Some side effects are tolerable, others are not, but most resolve themselves in a short period of time. Be alert to any unusual symptoms you may have in the days that follow taking the medication for the first time. Make a note of anything that doesn't seem right to you, and if you are worried, be sure to call the psychiatrist so that you can discuss it with him over the phone. You might need to see him for another appointment, and he may lower the dose, or change the medication altogether.

Many psychiatric medications cause upset stomach, tiredness, or dizziness. Most bothersome side effects are temporary, but if something persists be sure to call the doctor to see what he advises.

Trial and error

It is very difficult to get the right medication cocktail for bipolar 1, and most people take more than one or two medications to treat all the symptoms. It is difficult to treat the illness because of the various moods associated with bipolar – some medicines treat only mania and others treat only depression. Medicines must be tried out before a decision can be made. This can be a very long and harrowing process and can take weeks or months to get right in some cases. Then, on the other hand, some people find a medication that works the first time. If this is you, then you are fortunate.

Types of bipolar medications used

The types of medications frequently used in the treatment of bipolar are mood-stabilizers, anti-depressants, anti-psychotics, and medicines for reducing the symptoms of anxiety disorders that often accompany bipolar 1 disorder. Other medications may be used according to your psychiatrist's regimen.

I take a mood-stabilizer, three anti-depressants for depression and sleep, and an anti-psychotic in order to remain well. Luckily, I have finally found a combination of medications that works well for me, and I have not had a relapse in three years.

Finding the right medication for you

Unfortunately, it is not always possible to find the right medication at first as the side effects are sometimes too difficult to contend with. It may take trial and error before you find the perfect combination of medications to treat your particular symptoms. We are each unique and require different treatment. What works for me, may not work for you, so you will need to be patient and find the right combination.

Trying different drugs, sometimes for weeks or months, requires a lot of patience from you and your psychiatrist. Hopefully, you will eventually find the right cocktail. Once your initial symptoms have been medicated successfully, the drugs will continue to work as maintenance therapy to prevent relapses of your illness in the future.

Remembering to take your medications

If you have trouble remembering to take your medication, or if you are not sure if you have taken them or not, you might like to use an alarm, or a pill organizer that you can buy in the pharmacy. Also, some pharmacies use a system of packing all your medications into a special pill popper like bubble wrap so that you will know exactly if you have taken them that day.

This is a great idea, especially if you have a lot of medi-cines to take. If you have this problem, do ask your pharmacy if you can use this system.

Mood stabilizers

Mood stabilizers are medications that are used to stabilize bipolar 1 mood swings. They also prevent mood swings from occurring and lengthen the time in between them.

Lithium (Lithobid, Eskalith) was the first medication approved by the FDA to stabilize moods in bipolar 1. It was followed more recently by lamotrigine (Lamictal), valproate (Depakote, Depakene), carbamazepine (Tegretol), and oxcarbazepine (Trileptal).

Lithium (Lithobid, Eskalith)

This is a very old medication that was discovered by John Cade, an Australian researcher, in the 1940s. A naturally occurring salt, it was used to treat patients with mania who had been in mental institutions for years. It had a remarkable effect on their manic symptoms, and they were able to return home.

It took until the 1970s for the FDA to approve it for the treatment of bipolar disorder (then called manic–depression), and it has been used ever since with good effect on bipolar 1. Although other mood stabilizers have been introduced since, many doctors still like to use Lithium as a maintenance therapy.

Lithium is used today to control mania in bipolar 1 disorder. It is also effective in preventing recurrences of mania, depression, and mixed episodes. You may be given Lithium to bring your mood under control, then it can be used to stabilize your moods thereafter.

There is evidence that the use of Lithium can prevent suicide attempts and suicides, like I said previously.

Unfortunately, like many other medications, Lithium does cause several side effects, and these are sometimes serious. Lithium influences the thyroid and the kidneys, so regular blood tests need to be done to avoid this occurrence.

The other side effects are:

- Weight gain
- Dizziness
- Restlessness
- Dry mouth
- Tremors
- Digestive issues
- Swollen ankles
- Drowsiness
- Brain fog
- Metallic taste in the mouth

As with other medications, you will need to discuss the side effects with your doctor and weigh up the pros and cons of using Lithium.

You should not take Lithium if you have had:

- An allergic reaction to Lithium in the past
- You have heart disease
- Chronic kidney disease
- Low levels of sodium in the blood
  (this is caused by dehydration)
- Addison's disease
- You need surgery
- You are trying to get pregnant, are pregnant,
  or are breast feeding

Lithium usually takes ten to fourteen days to take effect on a manic episode. It is usually combined with other medications in acute mania because it doesn't take full effect for about six weeks. Hopefully, it reduces the number and severity of episodes of mania, depression and mixed states that might occur later.

It is available in two forms. Lithium carbonate in tablets or slow-release tablets and Lithium citrate, a liquid which is used for people who can't swallow.

It is very important when taking Lithium, that you get enough liquids and don't become dehydrated.

Lithium Toxicity

It is essential that your doctor keeps a close eye on you when you begin taking Lithium. You will need regular blood tests to make sure that the levels do not climb too high in your blood. Lithium toxicity is a medical emergency, and you should call you doctor or go to the emergency room if you think you have taken too much.

The symptoms of Lithium toxicity include:

- Upset stomach
- Nausea and vomiting
- Diarrhea
- Unsteady gait (walking)
- Light-headedness
- Slurred speech
- Delirium (This is when a person may be confused about their whereabouts and the date)

I was unfortunate enough to have Lithium toxicity one year. I didn't notice what was going on at first, but soon enough I was feeling very dizzy and could barely walk across the room. I went to the ER and was kept in for the night while they treated me for Lithium toxicity. I had five times the therapeutic level in my blood in only two weeks.

From that incident, I contracted high blood pressure and kidney disease, so you can see why it is vital that you have regular blood tests when you begin taking Lithium. I have since found a different doctor.

Valproic acid (Depakote, Depakene)

Valproic acid was originally used as an anti-convulsant for the treatment of epilepsy, but after several studies in the 1970s and 1980s it was found to be useful in treating the mood swings in bipolar 1 disorder. It wasn't until much later that the FDA approved it for acute manic episodes in bipolar 1 disorder.

Physicians have been using it for maintenance therapy of bipolar for many years now. It is used for mania and mixed features in bipolar 1.

Valproic acid can cause liver failure, in some patients, so frequent blood tests are usually necessary while taking this medication.

You should call your doctor or go to the emergency room at once if you have any of the following symptoms:

- Hives
- Vomiting
- Breathing difficulties
- Swelling of the face and tongue

As with all medications, Depakote has side effects. Some are more serious than others. Common side effects include:

- Nausea
- Vomiting
- Dizziness

- Headaches
- Tremors
- Blurred vision
- Hair loss

If you report these symptoms to your doctor, he will weigh the risks against the benefits of taking this medication. It may not be suitable if you are pregnant, and a safer medication might be found in its place.

Drink plenty of fluids while on valproic acid.

Lamotrigine (Lamictal)

Lamotrigine is often used to treat depression in bipolar disorder. It was approved for long-term maintenance therapy in 2003 by the FDA for this purpose in bipolar 1 disorder. It is also used to delay recurrent manic, depressive, and mixed moods.

This medication can cause a rare but serious skin rash, so must not be increased rapidly. The recommended schedule is: 25mg for two weeks, then increased to 50mg for two weeks, then 100mg for a week, then as prescribed by your doctor.

Other more common side effects are:

- Nausea
- Mild skin rash
- Vomiting

- Cough
- Dry mouth
- Constipation

Carbamazepine (Tegretol)

This medication is another anti-convulsant that has been used for many years in the treatment of acute mania and mixed episodes. It can be used alone or in combination with another medication, but due to its risk of serious bleeding conditions, it is not usually the doctor's first line of treatment.

Tegretol interferes with oral contraceptives, so a woman needs to use another form of birth control.

Blood tests are usually necessary when starting this medication.

Oxcarbazepine (Trileptal)

This medication is often used to treat bipolar disorder in the place of carbamazepine as the side effects are not usually as severe. Women need to be aware that, like carbamazepine, oxcarbazepine can interfere with the effectiveness of birth control medications, so there is an increased risk of unplanned pregnancies.

Atypical anti-psychotic medications

The newer, atypical anti-psychotics are usually used for bipolar 1. They can be used for short or long-term treatment of mania and psychotic symptoms such as hallucinations and delusions. Some are also used off-label as sedatives to treat anxiety, insomnia, and agitation. They are also useful in bipolar 1 depression, especially with psychotic symptoms.

Some are used to stabilize moods on their own, with patients who cannot tolerate Lithium or other mood stabilizers. They usually reduce manic symptoms quickly and can induce normal thinking in a few weeks.

The disadvantages with anti-psychotics are that they can cause considerable weight gain (sometimes 50lbs in three months), increased levels of cholesterol, and pose a risk for diabetes.

The common side effects of anti-psychotics are:

- Blurred vision
- Dry mouth
- Drowsiness
- Muscle spasms or tremors
- Weight gain

Tardive dyskinesia

Tardive dyskinesia (TD) is a very serious side effect of anti-psychotic medications, particularly the older anti-psychotics that have been used for a long time. Most psychiatrists treating bipolar 1 today do not use older anti-psychotics for this reason, but it has been found that there is still a low risk of tardive dyskinesia with the atypicals, the newer generation of anti-psychotic medications, if they are taken in high doses or for a long period of time.

Tardive dyskinesia is a muscle movement abnormality that may be irreversible if not caught immediately. The movements are mainly in the face, around the mouth, lips, and tongue, and include lip smacking, grimacing, tongue rolling, and jaw movements. It can extend to different parts of the body, and in extreme cases can be disfiguring and life-altering. Fortunately, tardive dyskinesia tends to be mild in most cases and is not disabling. However, it can be worrisome.

If you are on anti-psychotic medication this adverse reaction should be assessed by a doctor at least once every six months with the use of AIMS (Abnormal Involuntary Movement Scale).

There is no known cure for this serious side effect, but some medications are on the market to keep it under control. It is thought to be worsened during times of extreme stress. Two new medicines, Ingrezza (valbenazine) and Austedo (deutetrabenazine) have recently been approved by the FDA, but they are very expensive.

However, they can be obtained by a Patient Assistant Program from the manufacturers. If you should have tardive dyskinesia and stop taking anti-psychotics, there is the risk of the condition worsening over time, although, it may disappear altogether. Therefore it is important to catch it early, before it progresses.

Anti-psychotic medications

Here is a list of the anti-psychotics commonly used by psychiatrists today:

- Ariprazole (Abilify)
- Asenapine (Saphris)
- Cariprazine (Vraylar)
- Clozapine (Clozaril)
- Lurasidone (Latuda)
- Olanzapine (Zyprexa)
- Quetiapine (Seroquel)
- Risperidone (Risperdal)
- Ziprasidone (Geodon)

Anti-depressant medications

There is a lot of controversy around using anti-depressants to treat bipolar 1. It is certainly not the first drug that should be tried to treat bipolar 1 depression. In fact, a major study by the NIMH (National Institute of Mental Health) found that using an anti-depressant to treat bipolar disorder was no better than using a placebo.

What is agreed upon by all the experts is that anti-depressants should not be used alone to treat bipolar 1, but in combination with a mood stabilizer like Lithium, Lamictal or Depakote, or an anti-psychotic like Seroquel, Zyprexa or Vraylar.

Anti-depressants, especially the SSRIs like Paxil, Prozac, or Zoloft, must be used with caution when given to a person with bipolar 1 because they can trigger a manic episode. Many doctors do not prescribe them at all because of this unwanted side effect.

The SNRIs, like Cymbalta, Effexor, or Pristiq, are thought to be less likely to cause a manic reaction along with the tricyclic anti-depressants such as Elavil, Pamelor or Tofranil.

The medication Symbyax, (Fluoxetine and Olanzapine) is thought to be an effective drug for bipolar 1 depression, but still needs further studies.

The common side effects from anti-depressants medications are:

- Headache
- Nausea
- Sleepiness
- Agitation
- Loss of libido

If you are worried about taking your anti-depressant, you should consult your doctor. He may ask you to keep taking it, or stop your medication and taper it off slowly over a couple of months. Never do this on your own as you could be very sick.

Types of antidepressants:

- citalopram (Celexa)

- escitalopram (Lexapro)

- fluoxetine (Prozac, Sarafem, Selfemra, Prozac weekly)

- fluvoxamine (Luvox)

- paroxetine (Paxil, Paxil CR, Pexeva)

- sertraline (Zoloft)

- vortioxetine (Trintellix, formerly known as Brintellix)

- vilazodone (Viibryd)

Although there are serious risks when taking any medication, it must be said that the vast majority of people are able to tolerate psychiatric medications with no problems at all, and they are of great value to them in coping with the disorder. I have listed the serious side effects here more for your information, not to show you that the medications are dangerous.

Obviously, you are not expected to put up with side effects that are bothersome, especially after the first few weeks, so it is always best to keep your doctor informed if you notice that things are not quite right.

Chapter 23
Resistance to medication

Many people, when they are newly diagnosed, don't like the idea of taking medication in any shape or form. They just can't see the need for them because they, and other people they know, think that bipolar 1 is easy to manage.

It is sometimes hard to accept that bipolar 1 is a life-long condition, and there is no known cure. This means that, like heart disease, kidney disease, diabetes, and many other diseases, you must take medication on an ongoing basis to stay well.

The very thought that there is no cure for bipolar 1 makes many people rebel against taking medication at all, let alone for the rest of their lives. Yet, even though there is no cure, medication can help you live more productively. It is the first line of treatment in bipolar 1 disorder.

People who don't understand bipolar, think they can get better on their own if they can only find a way to snap out of it. They think correcting the symptoms of bipolar 1 lies within the person themselves, and if they would only make the effort, they would be able to get well. Misconceptions arise about bipolar 1 because some people are unwilling to accept that it is an illness that needs help with medication.

Stigma

There is also the valid question of stigma, of course, and many people quite rightly are afraid to admit to taking medication for fear that others will think they are crazy. Unfortunately, stigma is even rampant in the medical community, which makes the situation worse than it needs to be. Insurance companies separate physical and mental needs, as well, and mental illnesses usually come off badly and cost more money.

It is an indisputable fact that the stigma surrounding mental illness, particular bipolar disorder, is prevalent, and people are prone to judge somebody who has to take medication to function properly in society.

Suicide

Suicide is an ever-present danger in bipolar disorder, yet even this does not sway people's idea that if you could just try harder, you would be okay. If treatment had been more readily available, who can say how many deaths could have been prevented?

Other people think bipolar has something to do with the character, or even the personality of the person, which is totally inaccurate. Bipolar is a medical disorder that affects the brain and needs treatment just like any other illness.

You may not like taking a regular regimen of medication, but I think swallowing a few pills every day is far preferable to being sick with bipolar 1 mood swings.

As you know, mood swings can have a devastating effect on your life, and if you want to avoid this you need to remain on medication to prevent a relapse of symptoms.

As with all bipolar medication, do not stop or change the dosage without a doctor's permission as this can cause you to become very sick. Always carry a card with all your medications and dosages listed. Tell the doctor before having surgery or dental treatment.

Call the doctor's office if you should get an acute reaction to any medication. This would include things like:

- Hives
- Nausea
- Breathing difficulties
- Swelling of the face and tongue

What happens to people who stop taking medication?

It is so normal to want to quit taking medications that 70 – 90% of people with bipolar disorder will stop taking them at some point in their lives. Some stop taking them many times. The problem with this is that the illness is cyclical and always comes bouncing back, and sometimes the symptoms are worse than before. Then you have to increase your dosage, or even be admitted to the hospital to find a medication that works for you. When you stop taking the medication, you notice that your 'med holiday' ends only too soon.

If you are a person who has never taken a medication in your life, you might feel reluctant to take them for bipolar disorder. Yet this, and a stable lifestyle, are often the only way to feel well with this disabling disease. This applies more so with bipolar 1, as this form of the illness can make you feel very sick indeed.

Many people have a lack of support. This causes a lot of guilt and the person stops taking their medication altogether. It is a shame as they are doing their best to manage their illness.

Reasons for quitting

The most common reason people quit taking their medication is they can't see that they are sick. Denial is very common in mental illness. Bipolar often leaves you with a feeling that you are much better than you really are, so when you do start to feel better, you stop taking your medication. Of course, denial is counterproductive because it is the medications that are making you feel well!

Others think that medication will alter their creativity, or even their personality, which is a shame as being untreated means the disease will worsen over time. If you are worried about this, you may want to discuss micro-dosing with your doctor.

Some people do go without medication and remain fairly well, but for those cases I would say that their bipolar symptoms were not that bad in the first place – if they had bipolar at all. Certainly, someone with bipolar 1 would regret the decision to stop taking medication.

They are unaffordable

Also, medications are very expensive. If you don't have good insurance, it is sometimes impossible to be able to afford them in the first place. But there are other ways of obtaining medications that may cost you nothing at all.

Many doctors have samples in their office, and you only have to explain your difficulties to your doctor, and they can give you a supply for nothing. You can also investigate a Patient Assistance Program, as I have said before, to get your medications from the manufacturer. If you look up the company that makes the medication, call and ask for the Patient Assistant Program, then you will find that these companies are happy to supply you with free medication.

Side effects

Unwanted side effects are another reason people quit taking their medications, and there is no doubt that these can be very depressing. It is very true that several medications do have some unacceptable side effects like sleeping for fourteen hours a day, excessive weight gain, and some, mainly the SSRIs, even interfere with a person's sex drive.

Many people have brain fog which makes taking certain medications unbearable.

Anti-psychotics are often the culprits when it comes to weight gain. It is very demoralizing to put on a lot of weight, and can make you stop taking the medication altogether. But, once again, micro-dosing may work for you, and it is worth discussing this with your doctor. Some doctors and patients weigh up the pros and cons of taking the medication, even with weight gain, and if it is working for your illness, you may prefer to remain on it in order to feel well.

Gratitude for medications

As we all know, bipolar disorder has no cure, but it can be managed with medication and a diligent lifestyle. The way I look at it is to be very grateful that medications have been developed to treat my bipolar 1, otherwise I would be sick most of the time like I was before I was getting treatment.

If you can look at it this way, you will not mind taking medication, particularly if it makes you feel better. You certainly have a far better chance of living well with your illness.

Chapter 24
Supplements

When talking about a dietary supplement, we could be referring to one of the following:

- Vitamins

- Minerals

- Amino acid

- Dietary substance to supplement the diet by increasing the intake of enzymes or tissues from organs or glands

- Concentrate, metabolite, constituent, or extract

Not a lot of studies have been done on vitamins and various other supplements for bipolar disorder, and those that have been done are not altogether favorable.

Also, many studies contradict each other, so it is very difficult to know if what you are taking is harmful, or not. Some supplements can be dangerous and increase your chances of bipolar 1 depressive or manic episodes, as well as other serious illnesses. They can also interact with bipolar 1 medication or reduce their effectiveness.

One thing is certain, you cannot treat bipolar 1 with vitamins alone. Unfortunately, that is not possible. You will need to continue taking your prescription medications if you want to stay well.

The studies that have been done show that most vitamins can be found in the normal diet, so if you eat nutritious food, you will naturally get the vitamins you need. The only reason to supplement them is if you are on a restrictive diet for a period of time. And, even then, you would need to be very careful about which vitamins and supplements you take as some can have adverse reactions with bipolar 1.

The vitamins and supplements are as follows:

Omega-3 fatty acids. These are said to help moods over time, improve brain clarity, and lesson depressive symptoms, or the duration of depressive episodes. It is not recommended for manic episodes, so people with bipolar 1 need to be very careful when taking this supplement. Omega-3 fatty acids must contain EPA and DHA in order to be effective. The suggested dietary intake is 300 mg a day, but it must be cleared with your psychiatrist first.

It has been shown that people from various countries who have a diet of mainly fish, have a very low incidence of bipolar disorder. The lowest incidence was found in India, followed by Columbia and Japan. The United States has the highest rate of all.

However, you are always better off if you get fish oil naturally in your diet. These foods are particularly high in omega-3 fatty acids: Cod, salmon, sardines, and other fish.

Vitamin B1 is said to treat anxiety but is not helpful in mood disorders.

Vitamin B12 is not suggested for bipolar 1 but can be an energy booster, which can help with fatigue or side effects of sleepiness from some medications. However, most people get enough of this vitamin in their normal diet.

Magnesium is used successfully in anxiety, irritation, and insomnia.

Vitamin C is not recommended for people with bipolar 1 as it can induce mania and depression if you have too much in your blood stream, and most people get vitamin C in their diet.

Vitamin D does seem to have a link to bipolar disorder as many people with bipolar have a deficiency of Vitamin D. However, you would be wise to spend some time in the sunshine every day which will provide you with all the vitamin D you need. If you live in an inclement climate, you might care to invest in a full-spectrum light box.

Folic acid has been linked to bipolar disorder, but more studies need to be done on this supplement.

Some of the lesser-known supplements are **5–HTP** and **DHEA**. The body naturally makes DHEA until the person is in their mid-twenties, then there is a decline. Some people believe that an addition of this supplement can help de-pression (not bipolar 1) but the health risks of blood clots, heart and liver disease are always present.

Supplements to avoid

St. John's Wort (hypericum perforatum) has been used for mild depression for centuries in Europe, but again it is contraindicated for use with bipolar 1 due to the risk of mania. It also has conflicting reaction to anti-depressants.

SAM-e (S-Adenosyl-L-methionine) may also worsen mania.

Ginko biloba may nullify the effectiveness of bipolar 1 medication, particularly valproate acid (Depakote).

It seems that some of these supplements may help with mild depression, but most are contraindicated with mania. Just because something is said to be 'natural' it doesn't mean it is safe – **hemlock** and **nightshade** are natural, but they are both very poisonous. The rule of thumb is that if you want to take any supplements at all, be sure to clear it with your doctor first to avoid dangerous consequences.

Chapter 25
Psychotherapists and therapies

I always think it is desirable in the treatment of bipolar 1 to have a psychiatrist, and a therapist if you can afford it.

Bipolar 1 is such a complex diagnosis that you need a psychiatrist to prescribe your medications and a therapist to help you with the problems you face in your everyday life. Some psychiatrists do psychotherapy as well, but this is not common these days because therapy takes up a lot of time.

Short or long-term therapy

You may want to have a short-term treatment plan, or you may want to have an ongoing relationship with a therapist.

When you have bipolar 1, I think it is a good thing to be in therapy on a long-term basis as the illness is not going to go away. It is always good to have someone who will be on your side when you need help with the problems that will inevitably arise with this illness. But of course, time is money, so you must weigh up the pros and cons.

I have been with my therapist for the past twenty years, but as I live alone and have no family in this country, I need support for my illness. My therapist is someone I can share my life with, and he supports me in all my endeavors.

Psychotherapists

Psychotherapists often have a graduate degree, but some also practice with a master's degree. They each charge accordingly.

Finding a therapist is much like finding a psychiatrist. In fact, your psychiatrist may well be able to recommend one to you, or you can find one in the yellow pages or online.

Also, I have found that many churches have a psycho-therapy department, and the cost per session is usually low. They often take Medicare and Medicaid, as well.

Study the kind of therapy you would like first – we shall discuss this next – then call and ask if they do that kind of therapy. All therapists have their own way of working. They usually use the method they were trained in, but quite often they use an eclectic set of treatment plans because they will have gained experience of working with other people over the years.

Therapists all charge different fees. If you cannot afford them, and they do not take insurance, you may be able to see them on a sliding scale according to your income.

Your first appointment is the time when you can decide if the therapist is the right one for you. If you feel at all uncomfortable, you should not pursue therapy with that particular person because it is imperative that you can relax in their company.

You will be having many in-depth conversations about your life, and you will share some very personal information. Only by being with them for an interview, will you know whether you can work together. Hopefully, you will get a gut reaction, letting you know if they are the right therapist for you.

Various therapies

Talk therapy (Psychotherapy)

This kind of therapy is more informal than most and is based on your needs and concerns. It gives you a place to go where you can talk in confidence about your immediate problems and find solutions, as to how to cope with them.

Attention is given to past traumas, but in the main this kind of therapy focuses on what is currently happening in your life. You will be able to talk about your social life, your career, your marriage, your friendships, and anything else that is hampering your journey to wellness. Talk therapy is a way of accepting who you are and learning better ways to cope day to day.

You may have homework to do, or you may need to keep mood charts or a journal. These things will be discussed when you meet for the next therapy session to gauge your progress.

Here are some of the things you will be able to do better:

- Learn how to better cope with stress
- End risk-taking behaviors of bipolar 1 (like gambling, addictions, and sexual indiscretions)
- Define and work towards goals
- Make sense of past incidents
- Form a routine
- Plan for future crises
- Feel good about yourself

I must stress that to have a successful therapeutic experience, it is imperative that you find a therapist you feel comfortable with. If you don't click when you first meet them, you will know you need to find somebody else.

Cognitive behavior therapy (CBT)

This if often the therapy of choice for people suffering with bipolar 1 as the intention is to help you change your negative thinking patterns to positive ones.

CBT is done in a structured way over the course of a limited number of sessions – usually five to twenty. You will need to find out how many weeks the therapist usually works on this.

CBT is used for a wide range of emotional issues and mental illnesses, and helps you learn how to cope with chronic or acute challenges. The goal of CBT is to help you understand how thoughts and feelings can influence your behavior, which in turn gives you a positive or negative experience of the world.

Here are a few things that CBT can help with:

- Learn more about bipolar 1
- Prevent relapse of symptoms
- Learn how to cope with stressful situations
- Find ways to manage emotional problems
- Find ways to manage relationships
- Learn how to cope with past traumas from abuse and violence

CBT can be used on its own but is used in combination with medication when you are being treated for bipolar 1. Your therapy may be individual, groups, or groups with family members with similar issues. This can be discussed with your therapist, and you can both decide on which system would benefit you the most.

You will need to find out how many sessions you will need, the cost per session, and whether you can use a payment option. Some health insurance companies cover the cost of CBT, but you will need to find out if there are limitations on the amount of sessions you can have in one year.

Your first appointment

When you go for your first appointment, you may be asked to fill in some paperwork, or your therapist may ask you a few questions so that they can get to know you better. They may also ask you about your medical history and emotional concerns.

You may be asked to do some self-monitoring which means keeping track of your symptoms, behavior, and experiences. You can then share this information with your therapist so that he may help you with it. While you cannot control what goes on in the world around you, you will learn how to control your negative and unrealistic thought patterns.

You may find CBT challenging, and maybe even stressful, especially at first when you are learning how it works. If you feel upset, cry, or get angry that is quite normal, and an experienced therapist will be able to work with you on this.

Dialectical Behavioral Therapy (DBT)

DBT is an update from CBT, and was originally used for borderline personality disorder, a psychiatric condition for which there is no medication.

The sessions teach ways of coping with self-destructive urges like suicide, self-harm, gambling, drug, and alcohol abuse, overspending and so on. These skills are very useful in dealing with the impulsivity sometimes displayed by bipolar 1 patients, particular those in a manic episode. DBT treatment consists of skills training in mindfulness, distress tolerance, emotional regulation, and interpersonal effectiveness.

The sessions usually take place twelve weeks a year, with one month's break in between. The minimum commitment is one year, but most people keep going for at least two or three years because they find it very helpful.

Family Focused Therapy (FFT)

FFT includes the person suffering from bipolar, various members of the family, and friends. It is usually twelve organized sessions with a therapist. The therapy itself focuses on education about bipolar disorder and its effect on family and social life. The aim is to help the family understand what is happening to their loved one because of bipolar 1 disorder.

It aims at improving communication problems with you and your family, and teaching the family safe ways of problem solving. It teaches you how to look out for warning signs that an episode may be on the horizon, either averting it altogether, or preventing the situation from worsening. This therapy often enables you to cope better with your illness, lessening the episodes.

However, this therapy is usually only possible if you have a supportive family and many people with bipolar do not have that kind of support.

Interpersonal and Social Rhythm Therapy (IPSRT)

This is individual therapy centered upon stabilizing the daily rhythms of life. Most people with bipolar have problems with routines, so this kind of therapy is aimed at teaching better sleeping, waking, eating, and exercising habits. It works on specific attention to everyday problems and is not focused on past events.

(We shall cover all these topics in Part five).

Summing it up

By now you will know more about psychiatrists and medications for your illness. Hopefully, you will be able to find somebody you can trust if you haven't done so already. We have discussed medication in depth but be sure to ask your doctor if there is anything you don't understand. Always take responsibility for what you put into your body. Make sure it is right for you and not causing you undue side effects that are difficult to live with. See your doctor if you are not sure about this, or anything else to do with your medication, as it is of paramount importance in keeping you well with bipolar 1.

We have also discussed therapists and various types of therapy so you will be better able to find the right type of treatment for you. Here is a list of the topics we have covered in Part four:

- Psychiatrists and where to find one
- Medication
- Supplements
- Psychotherapists
- Various types of therapy

Family and friends

Hopefully, you are better equipped to understand bipolar 1 and your loved one's challenges by now. Finding a psychiatrist and a therapist can be very daunting, and many people feel great shame when having this illness.

Now that you know more about bipolar 1, you can be there to support them and help them see that good treatment is available. You can also encourage them to take their medications and not give up on them.

You will need to walk a fine line, though, as there is nothing worse than to be asked repeatedly if you have taken your medications at the least little sign of trouble. People with bipolar 1 have good and bad days, just like you and anybody else, and not every mood can be contributed to the illness.

Having a mental illness, let alone something as serious as bipolar 1, is very demoralizing and may well take your loved one a long time to come to terms with. You can encourage them to take good care of themselves and be open to learning new things about bipolar 1. You might even like to attend therapy with them if this is possible.

Unfortunately, you may not be able to contact the psychiatrist if they are an adult over eighteen, due to the HIPPA laws, but you can encourage them to keep their mental health appointments.

I realize that all this is very draining on you, and the rest of your family and friends. People can only take so much of bipolar 1 disorder, so don't be hard on yourself. Do your best to support your loved one, but always be open to

self-care as many caretakers become sick with the responsibility of having a person with this illness to look after.

You are doing a wonderful job just by showing an interest
in their welfare. Many people have nobody who cares
about them at all. So, thank you for being there to hold
their hand.

PART FIVE
LIFESTYLE CHANGES IN BIPOLAR 1

Chapter 26
Sleep and rest

All the authorities agree that medication is the cornerstone of bipolar 1. But you will find that lifestyle changes are important too. The other thing is, you are responsible for these changes which gives you a feeling of control over this devastating illness.

I never understand people who think just swallowing a little pill will be the answer to bipolar 1. It is great, yes, but it is certainly not where personal responsibility ends.

There are so many things you can do to help yourself. If you get a handle on bipolar 1, you will feel very empowered, so it is a good idea to start taking care of yourself right now.

Sleep and rest

You have heard me mention this subject a couple of times already, so you will know by now that sleep and rest are essential for maintenance of bipolar 1. In fact, it is a very important consideration, after medication, if you want to stay well and as free of symptoms as possible.

How we induce a regular sleep pattern is another thing entirely, and believe me I sympathize with anybody who has tried and failed many times over, as I found sleep very hard to come by when sick with bipolar 1. Then, on other occasions, I would sleep for eighteen hours a day, every day, when depressed.

The reasons for failure to get into a sleep pattern are many and varied, and it is well worth studying sleep and its effects on the body if you want to participate in your wellness plan.

The importance of REM sleep

REM (rapid eye movement) sleep is important to every-body, especially people with bipolar disorder. Yet REM sleep can be difficult to attain. Interrupted or absence of REM sleep can lead to many problems with bipolar 1, including relapse and hospital visits, so it is important to strive for REM sleep every night.

Deep sleep

Although REM sleep is good for you, researchers have found that deep sleep is even more important for keeping a steady mood. You may be in the unfortunate position of hardly being able to remember when you last had a night of deep sleep so may want to know what you can do to improve your situation.

Here are a few suggestions:

- Go to bed and wake up at the same time every day. Researchers have found that it is very important to stick to a regular wake up time, even if you haven't slept well, so set an alarm and get up as soon as you wake up. This should help improve your sleep.

- Go to bed and get up at the same time even on the weekends when you would rather lie in.

- Try getting at least fifteen minutes of sunlight a day, preferably in the early morning. This can help set your circadian rhythm (body clock) for the day. If you are not able to get sunlight naturally, try using a full-spectrum light box. This can be very helpful for people with bipolar, especially if you live in a northern climate where you don't get a lot of sunlight. You can find full-spectrum light boxes online.

- Work out daily if you can. Just ten minutes of exercise is better than none at all, but don't work out just before bedtime.

- Eat more fiber in your diet.

- Meditate, if you can, for five or ten minutes before bedtime.

- Avoid drinking any caffeinated drinks in the afternoon and evening.

  If you are going to drink alcoholic beverages, drink in moderation as alcohol may help put you to sleep initially but may well interrupt your sleep during the night.

- Avoid smoking two hours before bed as nicotine can keep you awake.

- Turn off the TV and do something relaxing half an hour before bedtime to put you in the mood to sleep.

- Take a hot bath or a shower.

- Read a book.

- Keep the bedroom for sleep and sex.

- Keep the bedroom dark – blackout curtains are good for this.

- Listen to white noise like the sound of the fan blades going round.

- Watch your weight as this can cause loud snoring or sleep apnea. Many psychotropic medications cause weight gain, especially the anti–psychotics, so be sure to eat a healthy diet and do some exercise every day.

- Take laptops and cell phones out of the bedroom as the blue light they emit on their screens can keep you awake. You might also be tempted to keep track of your emails when you should be sleeping!

- If you can't sleep, get up and do something relaxing in low light, like reading, then go back to bed when you feel tired.

- Take a power nap during the day by setting your alarm for thirty minutes of sleep.

Unfortunately, even with all these things you may still not be able to sleep, but it is something to strive for. So, practice every night, and be patient.

The quality of sleep is different in bipolar 1 depression and bipolar 1 mania. In depression, you often sleep too much. This is called hypersomnia, and you can sleep for fourteen to eighteen hours a day if you are extremely depressed. Some people sleep all day, get up for five minutes to go to the bathroom, then go straight back to sleep. Personally, I can't see anything wrong with over-sleeping as it seems to me the body is needing all that sleep during depression, but many authorities disagree with me and think you should strive to stay out of bed.

In bipolar 1 mania, it is hard to reason with anyone that they do in fact need to sleep. It doesn't seem as if sleep is important at all, besides you have far too much to do and can't waste time sleeping. But you can see that this is faulty thinking when you are well.

If you are prone to mania, you may not feel the need to sleep, but do try the things I have listed above as mania is induced and made worse by too little sleep.

Try Melatonin or magnesium

If you are having insomnia due to depression or mania, and are still unable to sleep, ask your doctor if you could take Melatonin. There is no evidence that this interacts with bipolar medications, but you may want to check with your doctor first.

Melatonin is quite potent and helps a lot of people sleep. The thing to be aware of is that you only need a tiny bit to be effective. If you take too much you are in danger of causing an insomnia rebound which can upset your circadian rhythm.

Magnesium is also good for sleep, but once again, you will need to ask your doctor if you should take it with your other medications.

Sleep Disorders Specialist

If you still can't sleep, you might like to see a sleep disorder specialist who may want you to do a sleep study. Many people have found they have sleep apnea and have been prescribed a C-Pap machine that lets them get better quality sleep instead of waking up several times a night to breathe.

See your doctor if you are kept awake by physical pain or restlessness. You may need tests to see what is causing this.

Cognitive Behavioral Therapy

Cognitive Behavioral Therapy can help some people with sleep disorders because it teaches you ways to stick to a strict sleep schedule.

Medication

If you are totally unable to sleep due to bipolar medica-tions, or even due to the symptoms of bipolar itself, you could ask your doctor for something to help you sleep.

Some doctors do not like prescribing medication for insomnia, but others will do so willingly as they realize how important sleep is to people with bipolar 1.

I have taken a medication for years now and have been able to sleep quite well. The problem is, even with this medication, I do sometimes have trouble sleeping as it is easy to become dependent upon it. It is not addictive, but you can build up a tolerance to it, then you need a higher dose.

I never fret when I have insomnia, these days, because I know it is a symptom of bipolar and it will soon pass.

Sleep journal

Try keeping a sleep journal so you can monitor your progress. It is good to look back and see the things you have done to improve your sleep and how they have helped change your pattern. You could record the times you go to bed and wake up and the quality of your sleep. This will give you some indication, over time, of whether your sleep pattern is improving or not.

Worries keeping you awake

Another thing worth mentioning is that people with bipolar 1 have a habit of ruminating, or endlessly going over their worries, especially at bedtime. This is very disruptive to sleep. Instead of letting your worries keep you awake, write them down before you get into bed. This tells the mind that you will tackle them in the morning so that you will be able to get to sleep. If you wake up in the middle of the night and find that you are caught up in the worry cycle, write them down or record them, then go back to sleep.

The importance of rest

This is something that is often overlooked in bipolar 1 disorder. Sleep is very important, obviously, but you also need to rest during the daytime. Very few people think of doing this, then get very tired and overwhelmed. Yet, if they took just ten minutes out of their day, they would feel much better.

Rest can be just sitting down with a good book, or making a point of lying down and doing relaxation exercises (more about that later). Whichever way you do it, rest is good for brain function, and to keep you from relapsing into mood episodes.

When I am feeling very tired, I put on some soft music and lie down for about twenty minutes. I close my eyes and just listen to the music for a while. I have some eye pads I bought online which are very good for resting the eyes. They are moist inside and can be heated up for ten seconds in the microwave. After twenty minutes of wearing them, I feel rejuvenated enough to get on with my day.

If you go to work, you might consider putting the passenger seat back in your car during your lunch break and just closing your eyes for ten minutes.

Muscle relaxation

You can also try resting with muscle relaxation. It is a very pleasant sensation and is easy to do. Try it now.

Simply lie or sit down in a quiet, comfortable place and close your eyes. Take some deep breaths. Now, when you are feeling calm, think about your toes. Picture your toes and feel them in your socks or shoes. Now scrunch them up as hard as you can and relax. Do this three times until your toes feel very relaxed.

Next take your attention up to your calves. Feel your calves and tense them up. Squeeze the muscles as hard as you can, then relax. Do this three times.

Do the same for your thighs, buttocks, stomach, chest, shoulders, back of your neck, biceps, and your fingers. Clench your muscles, then relax. Do this three times.

Clench and relax your jaw. Do this three times, as well.

By now you should be feeling better. You can rest, sleep, or simply get up and go about your day feeling warm and relaxed. It is very easy to do this when you are sitting, watching television. You can even do it when you are in a traffic jam. It will help you relax.

Chapter 27
Diet and recipes

Although there is no specific diet for bipolar disorder, or bipolar 1, there are quite a few guidelines that you might like to follow if you want to stay healthy. As you know, food is all important to good health, and this is particularly true when you have a mood disorder. Many people with mental illnesses have been found wanting when it comes to eating a good diet. Generally speaking, what you put into your body determines your quality of life.

Researchers agree that people with bipolar disorder suffer from more inflammation in the brain and a poorly regulated immune system, than other people, so eating the right foods may be the answer to this. It is always best to eat in moderation and eat a wide variety of different foods.

Inflammation is caused by many different factors. The American diet for one. We eat a huge amount of saturated fat, salt, and sugar in our diet, and all these things are bad for our health. If you can cut down on alcohol, get adequate sleep, and eat a healthy diet, you will have a better chance of staying well without mood swings. Not to mention living longer.

Obesity is another reason why people have a lot of in-flammation in the body and brain. Rather than try all the different diets and fail, it may be wise to see your doctor first and see if he has any suggestions as to a good diet for you. Also, if you are able, you might try going to a nutritionist who can prescribe a diet specially formulated for you. My motto is to eat in moderation then you can't go wrong. You can even use a small plate if that will help you cut back on food.

Many people who have bipolar 1 with mania, do not find the time to eat well at all, and often have a bag of chips for lunch. This is one reason why obesity is prevalent in bipolar disorder. As I have said already, some psychotropic medications cause obesity, particularly the anti-psychotics, so planning a healthy diet is of greater important if you are on any of these medications.

If you start out by eating a healthy diet when you begin medications that are known to cause considerable weight gain, you will be better able to cope with the inevitable cravings for sweet things.

People with bipolar disorder have many chronic diseases including heart, kidney and liver disease. So great care should be taken to eat a healthy diet, one rich in whole foods and lenient on sugar, salt, and fat.

It is very tempting to eat fast foods. You may eat them when you are manic or depressed for convenience and cost, but it is much better to munch on a fresh veggie and have a dip like hummus to make it tasty. You can also cook your food in bulk and keep it in the fridge. Then you will have enough for several meals. Or you can divide the leftover food and put it in the freezer.

Here are some foods and nutrients for good brain health in bipolar 1.

Omega-3 fatty acids

This plays a very important part in brain health, and does seem to help depression, but not mania. So far it has not been proven to be of help in bipolar disorder. However, it is good for the brain and the heart, so may well be worth incorporating into your diet. Try eating more cold-water fish as this contains the most omega-3 fatty acids. The fish with the highest levels are salmon, herring, sardines, tuna, mackerel, and trout. It can also be found in flaxseeds, flaxseed oil and eggs.

Whole Foods

Whole foods are foods that have not been modified at all, so this would include all fresh vegetables and fruit. Other foods such as whole grain bread, whole grain pasta, oatmeal, brown rice, and quinoa are also very good for your overall health.

Beans

Many different beans (legumes) are thought to reduce mania in bipolar 1. These include black beans, lima beans, chickpeas, and lentils, but all legumes are thought to be good for stabilizing moods. Beans can cause gas build up in the body, so introduce them slowly into the diet if you are new to eating them.

Turkey

Turkey is high in the amino acid tryptophan which calms the body enabling better sleep. It also helps to make serotonin which stabilizes the mood. If you don't like eating turkey you can get serotonin in tofu, eggs, and cheese.

Dark chocolate

We all know that chocolate is a comfort food, but dark chocolate is better for you if you want a calming effect for your bipolar 1 disorder.

Nuts

Almonds, cashews and peanuts are rich in magnesium which helps with stress and lowers cortisol levels. The magnesium content also helps with insomnia.

Probiotics

The millions of bacteria in the gut help prevent inflammation which is often present in depression.

Probiotics are also helpful in producing the stress hormone norepinephrine and the calming hormone serotonin. They can be found in live yogurt, kefir, kombucha, sauerkraut, kimchi, and miso.

Herbal teas

The herbal tea chamomile has been used as a folk remedy for centuries for upset stomach, anxiety, insomnia, and depression. Also, it has been found that sipping hot drinks has a calming effect on the body.

Saffron

Saffron is an Indian spice, and some studies have found that it works as well as some anti-depressants such as fluoxetine (Prozac). It is an expensive spice, though, so you might need to use it in small doses. It turns rice a beautiful shade of orange which makes it very satisfying to eat.

Selenium

This is a trace element that is essential for brain health. It also helps stabilize moods. It can be found in many foods such as Brazil nuts, tuna fish, halibut, sardines, shrimp, turkey, steak, beef liver and ham.

Foods to avoid

Unfortunately, there are many poor food choices available today and they usually fall into the category of convenience and comfort foods which we all love. That is why dieting is so hard for most people.

The foods we should avoid if possible are foods with saturated fats like red meat, and sugary, salty foods that are very tempting to eat. The only way to avoid all the cakes, pastries and salty chips is to not allow them in the house in the first place. Treat them as an unwanted guest!

If you are able, it is always better to shop on the periphery of the store and only go down the aisles for things like extra virgin olive oil, whole grain bread, brown rice, canned beans, and whole meal flour for baking. Eat foods on the periphery such as fresh vegetables, fresh fish, low fat yogurt, 1% milk, eggs, and lean meat like chicken or turkey.

Make a list of all the food you want to buy when you go shopping and stick to the list. That way you won't be tempted to put junk food into your cart, and you will save some money as well.

Some studies say that if you have bipolar, you are wise to avoid gluten, but this has not been proven. You might like to try a gluten-free diet anyway and see if your manic and depressive episodes are reduced or less severe.

Gluten free foods:

- Buckwheat
- Oats
- Millet
- Whole grain rice
- 100% whole wheat
- Whole grains

Gluten rich foods:

- Wheat
- Barley
- Rye

A diet that causes inflammation is bad for depression, so it is best to counteract this by eating foods rich in B vitamins and folate such as:

- Broccoli
- Spinach
- Brown rice
- Peas
- Liver
- Peanuts
- Asparagus

Omega 6

Ideally, our ratio of omega-3 to omega-6 fatty acids should be around 3:1, but there is more recent evidence to show that an even lower ratio of 2:1 or even 1:1 may be even more beneficial for the brain. Various foods are to blame for a high ratio of omega-6 in the body. These include such foods as:

- Corn
- Cottonseed
- Soybean
- Butter
- Fat cuts of meat
- Sausages
- Bacon
- Cheese
- Good low saturated fats:
- Canola oil
- Flaxseed oil
- Olive oil
- Cold water fish
- Leafy vegetables
- Nuts (especially walnuts)
- Flaxseed

The Mediterranean Diet

If one diet is good for bipolar, it would probably be the Mediterranean diet as it is rich in whole foods and low in saturated fats. Healthy food doesn't have to be boring, and if you eat well every day, it can transform your life.

The Mediterranean diet was originally formulated in the 1960s where it was based on the foods found in countries around the Mediterranean like France, Spain, Portugal, Malta, Italy, and Greece. The people who live in those countries were exceptionally healthy and had a lower incidence of chronic illnesses.

The Mediterranean diet is believed to slow the buildup of plaque in the arteries, preventing heart attacks and stroke. It also helps cognition, memory, dementia, and Alzheimer's in older people. It is also good for weight loss, preventing type 2 diabetes, and premature death.

We have already mentioned the type of foods that are healthy, and these include whole grains, fresh fish, lean meat, legumes, olive oil, fresh greens, fruit, seeds, and nuts. These foods are particularly delicious and are easy to prepare.

Recipes

I have included some simple recipes of mine for you to try. These recipes have been taken from the Mediterranean diet and adapted to my own way of cooking. They have few ingredients, and are easy to prepare, so you won't be overwhelmed when cooking them.

I love to eat, but don't like to cook much these days as I live on my own. So, these recipes are things I eat for convenience as they don't take long to cook. You might be like me, so would benefit by these meals. All the food is healthy and will make you feel better than if you eat convenience foods. I feel full and heavy when eating convenience foods, but these foods make you feel full but not uncomfortable.

From 1975 – 1978 I lived in Malta, a tiny island in the Mediterranean, and we were treated to wonderful fresh foods which form the basis of some of my favorite recipes. These meals are enough for two, but you can always serve them for two or three nights if you are eating alone. Or you can eat one meal and put the other one in the freezer to enjoy later.

All these recipes can be adapted to whatever foods you have in the house. You don't have to eat shrimp for the risotto, for example, you can easily eat chicken or turkey instead. And you can swap out the vegetables for those you have on hand. Be adventurous, think up recipes of your own, or you can find many online.

White bean soup

This tasty soup is wonderful in summer or winter, and very nutritious. I remember my husband's grandmother making white bean soup when we called in for lunch in Malta. We would be passing by, and she would be stirring a huge pot of this soup on the stove. She added parmesan cheese, but that is optional.

Ingredients

- 2 sticks of celery
- 1 large onion
- 1 large carrot
- 1 can of chopped tomatoes
- 2 cans of cannellini (white) beans
- 2 tablespoons of extra virgin olive oil
- 1 bay leaf
- pinch of oregano (fresh or dried)
- 1 pint of vegetable or chicken broth
- salt and pepper to taste (go easy on the salt)
- parmesan cheese (optional)

Method

- Heat the olive oil in a large saucepan.

- Finely chop the onion, carrots, and celery.

- Add to the oil in the pan and cook until soft. 5 – 7 mins.

- Add the can of tomatoes, the bay leaf, the oregano, the beans, and the vegetable broth.

- Season to taste.

- Bring to the boil, then simmer for 35 minutes.

- Serve with whole grain toast.

This soup should be rich and creamy, but if it is too thick add some hot water to the pan. If you like it thicker you can put it in the blender when it is cooked. Grandma made it thick, and you could stand your spoon up in it.

Greek salad

This is a delicious, filling salad to have on a hot summer day. The ingredients are bright and colorful, and it contains all the nutrients you need for a satisfying meal. They serve this salad in the open-air cafes in Greece and on the Greek Islands. It is very easy to make and doesn't need a lot of different ingredients.

Ingredients

- fresh spinach, cob, or romaine lettuce
- 1 pepper (green, red or orange)
- 2 fresh roma tomatoes
- 6 black olives
- 4 ounces goat cheese
- handful of walnuts
- handful of sunflower seeds
- extra virgin olive oil, balsamic vinegar, or lemon juice
- 2 slices of wholegrain bread

Method

- Wash the greens and pat dry on a paper towel. (If you have time, put them in the fridge for half an hour to crisp up.)

- Loosely chop the salad leaves and place them in a large salad bowl.

- Chop the fresh vegetables in large chunks and add to the bowl.

- Add the olives, walnuts, and sunflower seeds.

- Crumble the cheese on top.

- Toss the whole salad with a little olive oil, lemon juice, or Balsamic vinegar.

- Cut the bread into small cubes, toss in olive oil, and heat them on a baking tray in the oven until golden brown.

- Serve the croutons on top of the salad.

Chicken and avocado salad

A colorful array of nutritious ingredients along with chicken. Avocados are nutrient-dense and are often included in the Mediterranean diet. They are a rich source of fiber, healthy fats, vitamins C, E and B6, potassium, magnesium, and folate acid. You can eat this healthy salad for lunch or dinner.

Ingredients

- 1 large, skinless chicken breast
- fresh spinach or romaine lettuce
- 10 cherry tomatoes
- 1 or 2 avocados (depending on size)
- extra virgin olive oil
- salt and pepper
- honey vinaigrette dressing
- 2 tablespoons of extra virgin olive oil
- ¼ cup of balsamic vinegar
- ½ tablespoon of dijon mustard
- 1 tablespoon of honey
- ¼ teaspoon of oregano
- salt and pepper to taste

Method

- Put all the ingredients in a jar and shake until blended.

- Season the chicken

- Grill the chicken breast for 5 – 6 minutes a side. Then slice.

- Peel and slice the avocados.

- Arrange chicken, avocado and tomatoes on a bed of fresh spinach or lettuce.

- Pour the dressing over the salad.

- Chill in the fridge for half an hour before serving.

Spicy stir fry

I always love to eat stir fries as they are very easy to make and are always delicious. You can vary the ingredients to your taste and to what you have on hand. Yellow squash or zucchini are a big part of the Mediterranean diet and are versatile and easy to work with. You can make the stir fry without the sauce, but I love a thick coating of it on my food. If you prefer it without sauce, cook the meat and vegetables for a further 3 – 5 minutes.

Ingredients

- 1 large chicken or turkey breast
- 1 large onion
- 10 white mushrooms or one large Portobello mushroom
- 3 large yellow squash or zucchini
- 1 red pepper
- 2 tablespoons of extra virgin olive oil
- 1 cup of water
- 2 tablespoons of thick Szechuan sauce (or other thick Chinese sauce)
- ¼ teaspoon of salt

Method

- Season and thinly slice the meat.
- Chop all the vegetables into small pieces.
- Heat a wok or large skillet.
- Add the olive oil.
- Toss the meat in the oil on medium heat for 3 minutes.
- Add the veggies.
- Keep turning and tossing the food in the pan until cooked through but still firm. This should take about 3 – 5 minutes.
- Add the water and the sauce (mixed together) to the pan and cook the meat and vegetables for a further 3 minutes.
- Turn on high heat and stir. Be careful not to let the sauce completely evaporate. Cook until it is thick and creamy and clings to the meat and vegetables.
- Serve with brown or Basmati rice.

Italian mushroom risotto

Risotto is one of my go-to dishes when I have limited time or enthusiasm to cook. It is comfort food at its best, the rice being rich and creamy and the shrimp tender. I taught this dish to a friend of mine who has bipolar 1. She used to exist on junk food and frozen dinners. Now she eats risotto with all different ingredients. The secret to a good risotto is to always add HOT liquid to the rice otherwise it will halt the cooking process.

Ingredients

- 1 cup Arborio rice (no substitute)
- 10 mushrooms
- 1lb shrimp (peeled and deveined)
- 3 cups fish or chicken stock (preferably freshly made)
- 1 large onion
- 4 cloves of garlic
- 1 tablespoon of extra virgin olive oil
- 2 tablespoons of butter
- salt and pepper
- bunch of parsley

Method

- Heat the stock in a medium saucepan — keep hot. Add hot water if you run out of stock.

- Chop the mushrooms.

- Finely chop the onion and garlic.

- Heat the olive oil and butter in a large skillet.

- Add the onion and rice to the hot oil.

- Stir and cook until the rice is translucent at the edges. About 3 minutes.

- Add the chopped garlic and cook for 1 minute.

- Add the chopped mushrooms.

- Add some of the hot stock.

- Keep stirring and adding more stock until the rice is thick and creamy. This should take you 20 minutes. (You need to stir this dish continuously or it will stick to the pan.)

- Keep stirring until the stock is absorbed and the rice is tender.

- Season with salt and pepper.

- Add the shrimp and cook for a further 3 minutes or until the shrimp are cooked through.

- Finely chop the parsley and sprinkle over the dish.

- Serve with French bread.

Maltese omelet

When I lived in Malta, I was amazed at the fresh taste of all the vegetables, so devised this little dish that you can have any time of the day. It works well for breakfast, brunch, lunch, or supper. The secret to a good omelet is to cook it on medium heat or it will burn. When cooking the egg, lift the edge of the omelet with a wooden spatula and allow the runny white of the egg to flow into the gap.

Ingredients

- 6/8 large eggs
- 1 onion
- 1 red or orange bell pepper
- 1/4 bunch of green onions
- 2 sticks of asparagus
- 1 cup of grated mozzarella or Cheddar cheese
- 1/2 tablespoon of extra virgin olive oil
- salt and pepper

Method

- Beat the eggs. (Add a little water or milk if you like)
- Finely slice the vegetables.
- Heat the olive oil in a large skillet.
- Add the sliced vegetables and cook down for 3 – 5 minutes until firm but tender.
- Add the beaten eggs and swish over the cooked vegetables.
- Add the grated Mozzarella or Cheddar cheese
- Season with salt and pepper.
- Allow the eggs to cook and the cheese to melt for 5 minutes.
- You can either serve it as it is, or put it under the grill for a minute to further melt the cheese.

Marseille baked apples

This simple desert from the South of France will finish off any meal with panache. Baked apples are served in the little hole in the wall cafes in Marseille, and the warm, comforting smell of the apples is divine. So simple to make, yet so heavenly to eat.

Ingredients

- 2 large cooking apples (Grannie Smith)
- 2 tablespoons of brown sugar
- 2 tablespoons of raisins

Method

- Peel and core the apples.
- Arrange the apples on a baking tray or in a baking dish.
- Add brown sugar and raisins.
- Bake for 20 minutes on 350 degrees.
- Serve alone or with cream.

Ricotta brulee

Another easy-to-make desert that will blow you away.

Ingredients

- 1 tub of ricotta cheese
- 1 tablespoon of honey
- lemon zest
- 2 tablespoons of slivered almonds
- fresh blueberries or raspberries

Method

- Mix the ricotta and honey together in a small bowl.
- Pile into ramekins.
- Add the grated lemon zest
  (outer yellow rind of the lemon).
- Add slivered almonds.
- Broil until golden and bubbly.
- Add the fruit.

Food diary

If you are having a problem with mood swings, you might like to keep a food diary to see which foods are worsening your mood episodes.

Drinking water

Don't forget to drink plenty of water during the daytime. Fill up your container in the morning and sip it all day. If you don't like the taste of water on its own, you can add some lemon juice. Or you might like it better warm, or with ice. And always use a straw! You tend to drink more water when you use a straw.

Chapter 28
Exercise

In the past, I tried many ways to exercise but got nowhere. I was either bored or I couldn't get the hang of it. Everything I tried failed. Now I have joined a gym attached to the local hospital. I went there originally to do physical therapy for a limp, but have visited three times a week ever since. My limp is almost gone now, and I am fit and strong. I have to say, I feel much better than I have felt in years.

Now, I have changed my bad habit of saying, *"I hate exercise,"* to, *"I love exercise,"* which gets me to the gym every time. I don't like getting ready, but when I am there, I enjoy what I am doing. I get dressed and put on my sneakers early in the day then I am sure to get out of the house.

Seeing as I am in my seventies, I can only do so much. My rotator cuff was so badly torn in a car accident, it is now almost absent so I can't use my shoulder, but I do lift weights and do curls which is good for my biceps and triceps. To strengthen my legs and heal the limp, I cycle two miles, walk on the treadmill for twenty minutes, and do three rounds on the leg press. These are all good exercises for the heart, as well.

So, if I can do it, so can you. I will be your exercise buddy and cheer you on.

Exercise and you

You may well be an exercise junky already, so I don't need to preach to the choir, but if you are not, I would like to add some words of encouragement to help you feel well and prevent relapse.

If you are not one for exercise, I suggest you start out slowly by doing what pleases you. If you do not like the idea of going to a gym, by all means walk a little every day. You don't need to walk five miles, just a quarter of a mile will keep you fit every other day. Also, there is the bonus for people with bipolar 1 of getting all that fresh air and, hopefully, sunshine to help your mood.

You might try lifting some weights at home. They don't need to be heavy – start with 2 lbs. weights and build up to 5 lbs. or 10 lbs. If you don't have weights, try using cans of beans or packages of flour. They work just as well.

Another good exercise is dancing. There are heaps of dance videos on YouTube so you shouldn't run out of ideas. You could also join a dance class. My local activity center has line dancing, and I am sure that is great fun.

You might also like to try working all the muscles in the body by doing Miranda Esmond White's Classical Stretch videos. These are great exercises for keeping the whole-body limber.

If you are more energetic than me, you might like playing badminton, running, or swimming. These are all great exercises if you don't overdo it. Running can be very hard on the joints, especially the knees.

Some people find gardening good exercise. It is something enjoyable, and you can do it at your own pace whenever the weather is fine enough to stay outdoors. Other people just love to do housework and get their exercise from running the vacuum cleaner around the house. Housework is good for losing calories as well.

I am quite certain exercise will help your moods due to all the endorphins you will produce. It would be particularly good in the early stages of depression as it can give you a reason to get out of the house. I know it will be impossible if you leave it to the later stages of depression, so do it while you are still physically able.

One thing you must bear in mind is that vigorous exercise can exacerbate mania, and it can also keep you awake. Keep your exercise to a minimum if you feel that a manic episode is coming on. And, if you want to sleep well, don't exercise before going to bed.

To think I would be writing all this now, as only five months ago it would have been unheard of. I was definitely against exercise of any kind, but now that I am seeing the benefits, I am changing my tune. At least I can practice what I preach.

If you are still not convinced that exercise is good for you, try doing some of the following things:

- Walk the dog
- Park further away from the super-market entrance
- Read while using a stationary bike
- Walk up and down stairs
- Stroll around the park
- Take the stairs instead of the elevator

Unfortunately, people with bipolar 1 suffer more physical illnesses than the general population. They often have problems with:

- Obesity
- Diabetes
- High blood pressure
- High HDL cholesterol
  (the so called "good" cholesterol)
- High triglycerides (a fat in the blood)
  that is associated with bipolar 1.

All these illnesses can shorten your life. It has been found that exercise is good for preventing physical illnesses as well as mental ones.

Remember, the most important thing is that you enjoy your exercise sessions, so vary it as much as you can. Whatever you choose to do will produce those lovely endorphins, along with chemicals like serotonin, dopamine, norepinephrine which all improve your mood.

It is worthwhile taking a little time out a few times a week in order to stay well with bipolar 1, and it is amazing how just stretching the body really helps with your mood and reduces the chance of a relapse.

As with all exercise, if you are new to it, be sure to clear it with your doctor first so that you don't injure yourself. Also, listen to your body. If you are in pain, do not carry on with that particular exercise. Otherwise, enjoy your exercise routine.

Chapter 29
Yoga, Tai chi, and Qigong

Exercise is good for people with bipolar 1, but when you are feeling a bit manic you don't need something too vigorous as you will already be revved up inside. It is better to calm yourself down if you can by doing slow, contemplative exercise. The more you can relax with mania, the better off you will be.

Slow exercises with deep breathing are good when you are depressed, if you can bring yourself to do them. Depression wears you out, so a lot of exercise may be too much for you. But do try the holistic approach of mind, body, and spirit when you exercise. You might like to try one of the gentler forms like yoga, tai chi, or qigong. People in the East do not feel the need to pound the pavements, instead they do calmer exercises which keep the body supple and strong and the mind alert. These things are very important when you have bipolar 1.

Yoga

It is not to say that yoga is the answer to bipolar 1 mood swings, but it definitely has its place in your treatment plan. Yoga is physical and emotional, and involves disciplined movement, controlled breathing, and meditation. It has a calming effect on the body and leaves you feeling relaxed and invigorated at the same time.

While you are in a meditative state you can bring your attention to the pose and *"know"* that your mood swing is only temporary. Anything that is good for your overall wellbeing can help with bipolar.

Yoga is very popular in the West, nowadays, and you can nearly always find a yoga class where you live. If you can-not find anywhere to practice, do try YouTube videos.

I am not much good at yoga because I am not very flexible now, but you might be better suited to it than me. At least it is worth a try because it has so many benefits for bipolar.

I did try yoga when I was much younger, when I was more supple and had no chronic pain, but as I got older, I lost my enthusiasm and have not done it since. Don't let me put you off, though, as yoga is very good for you and easy for most people. Why not try it?

How to Practice

Here are a few poses (asanas) to get you started:

Dandasana (Staff Pose)

- Begin seated on the floor with your legs extended forward.

- Bring your hands alongside your hips and straighten your arms.

- Touch your big toes together and keep a small amount of space between your heels.

- Flex your ankles, drawing your toes back.

- Press forward with your big toe mounds. Rotate your inner thighs in and down and press down with your femur muscles.

- Extend your sternum away from your navel and broaden your collarbones.

- Draw the tops of your upper arms back while softening your front ribs.

- Hold the pose for 30 to 60 seconds and remember to breathe.

- To exit the pose, release your arms slowly and shake out your legs.

Ardha Pincha Maywasana (Dolphin Pose)

- Get down on your hands and knees on the mat.
- Keep forearms on the floor, shoulders and elbows parallel.
- Raise your back (spine) and buttocks as you tuck your toes. Keep legs straight. (An inverted V shape).
- Keep shoulder blades firm and raise your shoulders away from your ears.
- Walk your legs in towards your arms.
- Take 4 – 6 deep breaths. Hold for 30 – 60 seconds.
- Gradually come out of the pose.

Makara Adho Mukha Svanasana (Plank Pose)

- Lay on your front on the mat.
- Lean on your forearms, keeping them parallel under your shoulders.
- Tuck your toes under.
- Inhale and lift the body above the ground. Hold for 30 to 60 seconds.
- Exhale and come out of the pose.

If you have not done yoga before, please check with your doctor before you begin. Always take yoga poses (asanas) slowly. Don't rush, and deep breathe at the same time. You never hold your breath in yoga.

If you have any sign of pain, come out of the pose gently. I say this from experience because I strained my hip once and regretted it for quite some time. I learned the hard way that yoga, like other forms of exercise, is not meant to be painful, and once you feel tension you must come out of the pose. I would also advise you to find a teacher who has experience with teaching beginners.

Tai Chi

Tai chi (pronounced tie chee) is an ancient Chinese tradition that is still practiced today to relieve stress and focus on physical and mental wellbeing. It has evolved as a serious discipline, and you can still see whole families practicing in public parks every morning before going to school or work in China.

Tai chi (also known as tai chi chuan) is a subtle form of exercise involving a series of movements performed in a slow-motion, focused manner whilst paying attention to the breath. Each posture flows into the next without pause, thereby keeping the body in constant motion. There are many different styles of tai chi that pay attention to health.

Tai chi is a series of movements named for animal actions as in *"White crane spreads wings."* Breathe deeply and focus the attention on bodily motions. The movements are circular and relaxed in nature, and do not require fully extended limbs.

You may like to try tai chi as it is an inexpensive form of exercise that requires no special equipment, and can be performed indoors, outdoors, alone, or in groups. It is generally a safe practice, but if you are pregnant, have back or joint pain, you might like to check with your doctor first. But generally, you don't need to be in great shape to practice tai chi.

I actually did tai chi for a while, but I am not well coordinated so gave up. I imagine if I had stuck it out, I would have improved, and to be honest, writing about it now has made me want to do it again. I shall probably check out some YouTube videos and see what they have on tai chi now that I feel strong from going to the gym.

You do not need to believe in Chinese philosophy, but it might help you to know the concepts behind tai chi:

Qi
The energy force that flows through the body at all times. Tai chi aims at unblocking the centers and allowing the qi to flow unhindered.

Yin & Yang
Opposing elements, thought to represent the universe that need to be kept in harmony. Tai chi promotes healing and balance.

More research needs to be done as to the direct benefits of tai chi, but if performed correctly it can certainly be a positive influence on your overall health. If you do tai chi on a regular basis you can hope to see improvements in the following:

- Mood
- Depression
- Anxiety
- Stress
- Agility
- Strength
- Stamina
- Sleep
- Balance

How to practice

It is easy to learn how to do tai chi, but it is difficult to give you some examples of the movements as they all flow into one another. You can learn how to perform the movements on your own or in a class. Try watching YouTube videos on your own or learn in a group setting in activity or senior centers in town. Classes may be of short duration (say 12 weeks), or ongoing. If you want to make tai chi a way of life, ongoing classes will really help. Instructors do not need any special license or teacher's training to teach tai chi, but do ask them about their training and experience before you begin.

When you get serious about tai chi, you might like to practice in the same place and at the same time each day. That would be ideal, but I do know that with bipolar 1 your life can be totally chaotic, so even a few minutes here and there would be better than nothing.

You might also try practicing the movements in your mind when you are stressed out, such as when you are waiting in a doctor's office.

Qigong

This is probably not as well-known in the west, but it does have a growing following. Like everything else, I tried qigong. In fact, I did it regularly for five years at an activity center in town. I found it calming and stress-reducing, and really enjoyed the sessions.

We had a teacher who was very experienced and had done qigong for several years herself before teaching it to a class. She was very knowledgeable and was able to combine certain practices to make it more interesting.

At the beginning of the session, we had to state our intention for that day, and I have to say, I never remembered what my intention was after the class! But nonetheless, I really enjoyed going and think of going back sometimes. But I always move on to other things in life, so have given qigong a miss for now.

If you haven't come across qigong before, I have to tell you it is very enjoyable and not demanding at all. Anybody can do qigong. It doesn't take any special skill. Yet, again, I must emphasize, you should see a doctor before doing any form of exercise.

Qigong is roughly translated as "master of your energy:"

Qi – the vital life force

Gong – mastery or cultivation

Qigong (pronounced chee gong) is another form of mind, body, spirit practice that focuses on deep breathing and movement. It is similar yet different to tai chi in that the movements are purposeful and repetitive, and many are done for a certain number of times, say 5 to 10.

The postures do not flow as in tai chi but are stationary and mindful.

The aim is to put all your focus on a particular body part to increase the flow of qi. The qi energy makes you feel alive and vibrant and opens that particular part of the body and gives it strength and balance. It is said that the qi energy goes where the mind is. What you concentrate on becomes your reality.

Feeling the life in your feet

My therapist does not claim to do qigong, but he does use certain techniques that are very like qigong movements in his practice. One of them is to bring all your attention to your feet. Feel them on the ground and wiggle your toes. Now focus on your feet and feel the life within them. Feel the warmth, tingling or pulsating of the toes. Feel that they are alive.

If you do this while sitting down, you will see that it brings your awareness to parts of the body you never think of which is very good for bipolar 1 because it takes your mind off what is bothering you.

Active or passive qigong

You can do active qigong (Yang) or passive qigong (Yin). Both are beneficial. The active form involves standing, controlled movements and deep breathing. The passive form is done standing or sitting still and focusing on active breathing. It also includes meditation.

Either form brings awareness to the body. Qigong is said to be helpful in calming anxiety or stress. It is also used to prevent chronic diseases like diabetes and heart disease, and to promote muscle strength, lymph drainage and focused awareness of the body space (proprioception).

Like all the ancient Chinese energy practices, qigong needs more research to substantiate its claims, but for now you could try it to calm your mind when you are anxious or under a great deal of stress.

How to Practice

Let us take a couple of beginner's poses. These are often used at the beginning of a session to wake up the body before doing more advanced poses. They are very simple and can be done by anybody.

Gentle Sway

This is my favorite pose as it really loosens the body and mind and makes you feel relaxed and energized at the same time.

- Stand with your feet shoulder width apart, arms hanging loosely at the sides of the body.

- Begin to sway your arms across your torso, letting the backs of your hands tap your torso in the front and the torso at the back.

- Twist at the waist as you do this swaying motion.

- Imagine you are wringing out a washcloth.

- Do this for ten to fifteen minutes to warm up.

The Bounce

This is a gentle pose also used as a warmup exercise. It is very simple to do, but very effective.

- Stand with your feet shoulder width apart. Knees slightly bent.

- Arms hanging loosely at the sides of your body.

- Bounce your knees gently up and down. They should feel loose and empty.

- This is the zero position for the body and should feel deeply relaxing. Do this for one to three minutes.

Both the above poses are designed to massage the internal organs for longevity. If you think you might like qigong, see if you can find an instructor where you live, or you might try some YouTube videos instead.

Chapter 30
Meditation and creative visualization

Meditation

Everybody will tell you that meditation is good for people with bipolar 1. And yes, it is great to be able to focus on one thing, but as we all know, bipolar 1 symptoms can be all over the map, and it is not often you can be in the zone.

If you are depressed, your whole concentration is on how bad you feel, and the thought of totally concentrating on one thing seems impossible. Besides the fact that when you are depressed you can only think of negative things, mostly directed at yourself. So, meditating while depressed is difficult, but not impossible.

Meditating while you are manic is more difficult. You are far too busy changing the world to meditate. So, once again, bipolar mood swings win out, unless you can slow down for a few minutes.

If you are really lucky, and have a euthymic window between mood swings where you are not experiencing any symptoms at all, by all means learn to meditate. It is good for you. Also, if you learn during a euthymic period, you may well be able to carry it over to when you are sick.

That being said, when I was having ultra-rapid cycling episodes for weeks on end, I had no interest in learning how to meditate, but now that my symptoms seem to have gone away altogether, I have found time.

I am taking advantage of this dry spell to meditate once a day for five minutes. Believe me five minutes is a very long time and I don't always make it, but I do try. If you can meditate for more than five minutes, you are much better at meditating than me.

Some people with bipolar 1 meditate every day, come rain or shine. It becomes a habit. I am envious of them because there is no doubt about it, meditating does make you feel better and more relaxed.

It is strange how concentrating on one thing for a period of time can make you relax, but that is the way it is. Most devotees of meditation say they feel happier in their lives. Anything you can do to calm the chaos of bipolar 1, the better. So, if you are interested, I shall help you begin.

Learning to meditate

First things first, you will never be able to meditate if you have a house full of screaming children, or someone who likes to have the TV on loudly all day. You need total peace and quiet to focus your attention. If you live with other people, try to carve out some time to yourself.

Next, you need a suitable place to meditate. You should make sure you are not too hot or too cold, you find somewhere comfortable to sit or lie down, and you are not too far away from an object as to strain your eyes.

Personally, I cannot meditate if my room is untidy. I have to pick up before I can even think of beginning, and this may apply to you, as well.

Decide to meditate for one minute. That may not sound like very much, but believe me a minute is a very long time when you are keeping your focus on one thing. You can always increase your timing later, but for now settle on a minute. Make it a game.

Choose something to focus on. I often concentrate on a candle – the flame is mesmerizing as it flickers on the wick. Be sure to breathe deeply while you are watching. Never hold your breath in meditation.

Another way is to focus on your breathing. Do not try to change your breathing, just breathe naturally, and think about your inhalation and your exhalation. Breathing in and breathing out. Calm and slow.

Breathe in to the count of five, hold your breath for a count of seven, then breathe out to a count of five. In and out. Five, seven, five. If you can manage a minute of meditating, you will begin to relax.

My very favorite way to meditate is to lie back on the bed and visualize nice, fluffy clouds in a blue sky. I take deep breaths and watch the clouds pass by. I may even see some shapes I recognize, but if not, I just watch them form and disperse, and move across the sky. This is very relaxing and works every time for me.

You are probably like me and have thoughts continually bombarding your mind. That is why it is good to watch the clouds form and disperse. They are your thoughts, and you don't have to pay them any attention at all. Just let them come and go. Don't judge, don't think about them at all. Just let them pass by in your mind like the clouds.

When you get used to meditating for one minute, you might like to try two minutes. Then you can build up to five minutes, and so on. Some people can even meditate for twenty minutes, or longer. I am not sure how they do that, but I don't think the length of time is necessarily important. The most important thing with meditating is the breathing. Keep it slow and rhythmic. Inhale deeply, exhale deeply, and you will begin to feel better.

There are hundreds of ways to meditate. You can find all kinds of different things to do in various books on the subject. However, in the end, it is up to you to find something you are comfortable with. Try to practice daily, at the same time each day. Feel the deep relaxation wash over you.

Creative visualization

If you are wondering what creative visualization is all about, think of the name. It is seeing something in a creative way. You can get great videos on YouTube about creative visualization, then you will see that there are hundreds of ways of doing it, as well.

Creative visualization used to be a fad in the 1990s, and no doubt some of you will remember this time period. I remember having a few friends round to share the visualization with, and it was great fun. I have a calm voice that lends itself to this method of relaxation. One friend, who also has bipolar 1 and anxiety, would come round to see me whenever she got stressed out, and I would do a creative visualization exercise for her.

Practice this as often as you can, and you will begin to feel better whatever mood you find yourself in. Remember to breathe deeply and take it very slowly. Never rush.

Here are a couple of exercises for you.

Market stall with fruit and vegetables

Choose a quiet, comfortable space for meditation. You may sit or lie down. Close your eyes and take deep breaths until you feel relaxed. Now imagine that you are in a produce market in town. The stalls are piled high with fruit and vegetables of every description. There are apples, oranges, melons, bananas, and all kinds of fresh, vibrant vegetables like red peppers, green peppers, radishes, and cucumbers.

Now, it is time for you to buy some fruit and vegetables for yourself, so you choose a basket and walk around the stalls. The first thing you come to is the honeydew melons. They are piled up in front of you. Pick up one of the melons from the pile and hold it in your hand. How does it feel? Is it light, or is it heavy? Does it feel pleasant in your hand?

Inspect the melon and see what color it is. Is it ripe? Press ever so gently with your thumb to see if it will give a little at the top. Now, bring the melon up to your face and smell the fruit. What does it smell like? Describe the smell to yourself. Now put the melon in your basket and walk on to the next stall.

You are now standing in front of the red peppers. Pick one up and feel it in your hand. Describe the weight, the color, and the ripeness of the pepper. Note the shiny skin, then smell it for yourself.

Do this with other fruit and vegetables until you feel very relaxed indeed. Take some more deep breaths, then slowly open your eyes. You should feel nicely mellow and rested.

End of visualization.

Walk around the park

Another creative visualization I like to do with friends is what I call a walk around the park. We have an interesting city park down by the river where I live and there is a lot to see, so it is easy to make up a narrative as you work on the visualization. Even if you don't have a park where you live, you can always conjure one up in your mind and find that you can visualize it well.

Start off by lying or sitting down, close your eyes, and take some deep breaths. Now imagine you are in the car park down by the river. Get out of your car and pick up your mat from the trunk. Now you are ready to take a leisurely walk in the park.

It is warm and sunny, and you can feel the warmth of the sun on your bare arms.

Leave the car park and picture yourself walking down the path towards the river. Notice the grass on either side of the path and the flowers that are growing wild. They are red, yellow, and white. Picture them clearly in your mind's eye. You see some white roses and smell their petals. Describe how they smell.

Now it is time to move on and cross the bridge over the river to get to the little island in the middle. You are standing on the bridge now and can see down through the clear water. You see many different fish swimming by. You count them as they duck under the bridge. You even see some turtles on a log. As you walk past them, they jump off the log with a loud plop into the river.

There are some ducks on the river. You see that they are a family of mother, father and six baby ducklings. You watch them swim by and pay attention to their beautiful feathers. You see the colors and imagine how they would feel if you could touch them.

It is time to move on to the little path that runs alongside the river. You see that there are huge cypress trees arching over the river. In fact, there are cypress trees all along the riverbank. You watch their leaves blowing in the soft breeze.

You see a few men fishing on the riverbank. You shout out to them as you pass. They call back to you and tell you about the fish they have caught today.

It is time to sit down on your mat at the river's edge now. You smell the freshness of the newly cut grass and watch some swans float by. You see the water lilies showing off their creamy pink flowers at the edge of the river. After a few minutes of relaxation, you pick up your mat and walk back along the riverbank towards the bridge.

The ducks have gone from under the bridge now, but the turtles are still there on the log. They plop into the water as you walk by. Now you are back on the little path that heads towards the car park. Once you get back to your car, you place your mat in the trunk and go and sit in the driver's seat. You now take a few deep breaths and open your eyes.

End of visualization.

You can visualize all kinds of scenes, real or imaginary, take walks through the town or up in the mountains. Take other walks on the beach or the forest. You can go wherever you wish in your mind's eye. This type of relaxation is very good for bipolar 1 symptoms because it calms the thoughts in your mind.

You can either get someone to read this mediation for you, like I do for my friends, or you can record yourself speaking it, then play it back to yourself when you want to relax.

Chapter 31
Mindfulness

You will no doubt have heard of mindfulness, as it is really in vogue just now. Many books have been written about it, and many videos are available if you want to try out different techniques while someone is guiding you. The Buddhist monks practice this as a way of life.

Again, this is very helpful if you have bipolar 1 as it helps concentrate the mind and focus on what you are doing during the day. In fact, when you are proficient in your practice, you may well find you are having less mood swings because it is very relaxing.

Whether or not you can concentrate for long periods of time will be something personal to you, but even practicing for fifteen minutes will help your equilibrium. It would be particularly helpful in depressive episodes as it takes your mind off the eternal self-blame. You may have difficulty doing it in mania, though, as like all these other calming exercises, it is difficult to concentrate on anything at all when you are manic.

The idea is to bring your mind purposely to what you are doing and pay attention to every little detail of each task. If you are eating, walking, resting, even breathing, you pay attention.

Everything is slowed down in mindfulness so that you can concentrate on what you are doing. No rush, no hurry, just watch what you are doing and pay attention. It takes practice because it is difficult to slow down in this busy world we live in. We are so used to rushing from one activity to the next, our mind on something else entirely.

Sweeping the floor

I have dabbled in mindfulness and found it helpful in slowing down the thoughts and taming the emotions. Once, when visiting my friend in Italy, she asked me to sweep the floor before the arrival of her guests for a party she was giving. You will understand that this was no normal floor, it was a marble floor the size of a hotel lobby as she has a very big house and plenty of money. She also has a very big broom — about four feet wide.

So, as I had nothing better to do, I took on the task of sweeping the floor, and decided to do it mindfully. This meant I paid acute attention to everything I was doing, sweeping slowly from side to side, feeling the handle of the broom in my hand, and listening to the swish of the broom's bristles on the marble floor.

It took a very long time to finish the floor because I was studying every single sweep of the broom. My friend was surprised and commented on what I was doing. I told her I was sweeping mindfully, and I felt as if I was at one with the broom and the motion.

Buddhists have a saying that describes mindfulness. *"Chop wood, carry water."* When you are doing those things, you concentrate on every aspect of the action and think of nothing else. This is called living in the now.

You may not have a palatial house and a hotel-size lobby like my friend, but you could do the following exercise several times a day:

Washing the hands

- Stand at the sink and turn on the faucet.

- Slowly run your hands under the running water and watch as it splashes into the sink.

- Turn off the faucet.

- Now take the soap and lather it up in your hands. Pay particular attention to the bubbles that form and the smoothness and the smell of the soap. Breathe in deeply and savor the delicate smell of the soap.

- Turn on the faucet again and rinse the soap off your hands. Feel the water rolling off your fingers.

- Turn off the faucet.

- Take up the towel and dry your hands. Feel the cloth on your fingers, palms, and the backs of your hands.

Other practices

You can use mindfulness for many other things as well. Many people use it for scanning the body, but this is not part of your everyday experience as you have to purpose-fully stop what you are doing to do this exercise. It can be very beneficial when you are feeling stressed or anxious:

Body Scan

- Lie down on the bed, with your palms facing upward and your feet slightly apart.

- Lie very still and become aware of your breath. Do not try to change your breathing in any way, just follow the breath in and out. Pay particular attention to the temperature of the breath entering the nose, and the temperature when it leaves your mouth.

- Now it is time to scan your body from your toes to the top of your head. This is similar to what I told you my therapist does as it is paying attention to how alive the body is.

- Take your attention down to your feet and just picture them in your mind.

- Scan the toes and the bottoms of your feet, then slowly move on up the body.

- Scan the calves, the knees, and the thighs.

- Buttocks and pelvic girdle.

- Stomach and lower back.
- Chest and upper back.
- Shoulders, upper arms, elbows, and lower arms.
- Hands and fingers.
- Back of the neck.
- The face, eyes, nose, and mouth.
- The top of the head.
- When you reach the top of your head, take deep breaths, and slowly open your eyes.

Chapter 32
Having fun

When people write about the things you can do to help live with bipolar 1, the last thing they write about is having fun. Isn't that terrible? Think about it. Bipolar 1 is a devastating illness that is very hard to cope with. We all know that. You need to educate yourself on all the ins and outs of the disease in order to cope at all. Isn't that bad enough? So, why shouldn't you have some fun now and then?

I know it is very difficult to even consider having fun when you are experiencing mood swings. Nobody said it was easy. But the rewards are amazing. To take your mind off your problems, for even a little while, can be very energizing. If you are in the depths of depression, you will obviously not have the motivation to do anything at all. That is understandable as lack of motivation is part of the illness. But if you try to have a bit of fun when you start going into a depression, can you see how helpful this would be to halt the progress of the depression?

We are also wary of having fun when manic because mania is all about fun anyway, most of the time, unless you have dysphoric manias. Risks are taken in many different areas which means that we should not encourage a person to have more fun!

But during the euthymic periods of bipolar 1, you may well like to devote some time to having fun. It is good for you. It is a tonic, a pick-me-up, that will keep you well for longer periods of time.

I must admit, I am fairly new to this concept myself. I was under the impression that once you were an adult, your play time was over. I thought play was for little kids. But I couldn't have been more wrong as playing when you are an adult is great. I love it now that I have learned how to do it.

Once, when I went to see the nurse at the clinic on my usual appointment to see the psychiatrist, she asked me what I did for fun. I was shocked! What on earth was she talking about? I have bipolar 1, don't I? People with bipolar 1 don't have fun.

I suppose that was the way I was brought up, and my parents certainly never had a day of fun between them. Life was hard. It was drudgery. Moving from one boring task to the next. I had to be serious about life, surely?

But she got me thinking, and I did contemplate having some fun in the future when I was well. That time never came for a long while because I was sick with ultra-rapid episodes and couldn't get off the roller-coaster if I wanted to.

However, when I found the right medication, I did decide to have some fun. I tried several things and was amazed at how well it made me feel. I felt young again and it was great. I have to say, I looked over my shoulder a few times, just to make sure nobody was watching me!

So, if this is you, please drop that idea. Life is hard enough with bipolar, you need a break. Imagine you are a child again and doing all the things a child loves to do.

Here are some things you can try to bring a little light-heartedness into your life:

- Paint
- Draw
- Sing
- Origami
- Zen tangles
- Dancing
- Hiking
- Camping
- Pottery
- Flower arranging
- Crossword puzzles
- Jigsaw puzzles
- Online card games
- Social groups
- Listening to music
- Playing a musical instrument
- Sports
- Cycling
- Swimming

The list is endless! You can add many things to my list, I am sure.

I also recommend adult coloring books as they are very relaxing. I began using coloring books, then decided to upgrade my pencils and do some real drawing. There are many colored pencil boards on Pinterest and several people on YouTube offer colored pencil classes. I also paint in oils, do acrylics and watercolor. Best of all, I like collages. I can recommend any of these things, even though art supplies are often expensive. The thing about colored pencil is that they are very reasonable for even a good set, and an adult coloring book doesn't cost much these days. Or you could always use an ordinary pencil and paper to draw things you like. Those cost very little indeed.

Whatever you decide to do, be sure to have some fun in your life. Smile, even laugh. There is nothing like a good belly laugh for making you feel better. Believe it or not, if you make a special effort to lift the corners of your mouth when you are depressed, it will instantly relieve your stress.

I know smiling is the hardest thing to do when you are hardly able to clean your teeth but try it. Just do it. You will be amazed at the difference it makes to how you feel.

Summing it up

Part 5 has been long and varied. We have covered a few topics, and I hope they have been of some help to you. Many of the things I have talked about will be familiar to you, but some might be new. It is good to open your mind, expand your horizons, and think of all kinds of things you can do to make yourself well.

I do hope you will try some of the things I have mentioned here. I have no doubt that you will feel much better if you do.

I have great faith in you. I know you can do it. Just smile.

We have covered the following in Part 5:

- Sleep and rest
- Diet and recipes
- Exercise
- Yoga, Qigong, and Tai Chi
- Meditation and Creative Visualization
- Mindfulness
- Having fun

Family and friends

You will know by now that there is more to bipolar 1 than suffering. It may be a revelation to you.

We have discovered that it is not enough to pop a pill into your mouth and expect to be well all the time. We have to take responsibility for our illness.

So, after you have read this chapter, you will be able to see some things your loved one could do to improve their life. You will be able to help and encourage them to do them. You may even think of doing some of the things with them. Whatever you do, know that your loved one is doing the best they can with the challenges they are facing.

I do hope you are taking care of yourself, too.

PART SIX
MANAGEMENT OF BIPOLAR 1

Chapter 33
Daily wellness plan

I will start this chapter by talking about WRAP then show you how I have adapted it for my own use.

WRAP stands for Wellness Recovery Action Plan, and it is very valuable for any work you decide to do to feel better with bipolar 1.

I have done three courses of Mary Ellen Copeland's WRAP and have found the whole concept very useful. It took me rather a long time to understand what I was doing, I must admit, because I am inclined to see the trees and not the forest. But when you can see the forest instead of the trees you will have a greater chance of success with this plan.

The basic concept is that you are responsible for your own illness. Therefore, you must do all you can to stay well. You are the master mind, and all the things suggested in the WRAP plan are at your fingertips. I envision it in the shape of a wheel. The hub is you, the Manager of your life, and all the spokes are the things you can do to get well and stay well.

You may benefit from studying Mary Ellen Copeland's WRAP on your own, or you may be lucky enough to find a course that would suit you in your community. I attended these courses at my mental health clinic, and if you have a clinic in your area, you might ask them if they do a WRAP program.

However, I had a problem with not seeing the forest for the trees, like I said, so had to modify the plan to suit my kind of lifestyle and symptoms.

I took a binder, called it my Daily Wellness Plan, and labeled the dividers into the following sections:

- **THINGS TO DO EVERY DAY**
- **DEPRESSION**
- **MANIA**
- **ANXIETY**
- **PANIC ATTACKS**
- **TRIGGERS**
- **PAIN (physical)**
- **PSYCHOSIS**
- **CRISIS MANGEMENT**

These are my challenges, so they may not reflect yours at all. You will need to develop your own plan, but it is something for you to think about. If you recognize these headings as pertaining to your particular challenges, feel free to use them. I use this binder daily to keep me feeling well. It has been invaluable.

Once you have your dividers labeled in your binder, introduce a number of lined pages into each respective slot. Take each section at a time, and write down all the things you can think of doing to stay well. We have discussed many things that may well fit in your binder, so use them to advantage. You will, of course, find other things I haven't thought of. Once you have done that, you will have something to refer to should you begin to get sick.

Under depression, for example, you might write down all the things you do at the moment to keep from being depressed, as well as all the things you might like to try in the future. Then, when you feel yourself getting a little depressed, reach for your plan and see all the things you could do to avert another depressive episode.

The same goes for mania. In that particular slot you could enter all the things you must look out for in the prodromal phase of mania, and the things you could do to avert another episode.

If you want to be successful with this plan it is best to keep your Daily Wellness Plan binder out where you can see it. If you put it up on a shelf, you are likely to forget about it for weeks at a time and it needs to be done every day. Use a colored or patterned binder so that you can recognize it easily and don't lose it.

Whether you start the day by looking at your binder, or finish the day by checking off what you have done, is irrelevant. The thing is to remember to use it.

If you are lucky, you will begin to see patterns emerging in your daily challenges which can be very helpful.

We shall discuss mood charts later, but this would be an ideal place to file them.

I have included crisis management in the plan, which is obviously very important, and I shall talk about that later. I hope you are never in crisis, but if you are, you can retrieve your plan and take immediate action. I am sure you will find it very helpful and will do a great job of using it.

Chapter 34
Routines

Many psychiatrists say bipolar disorder is a circadian rhythm disorder. Our circadian rhythm is like a body clock telling us when to sleep, when to wake up, when to eat, and when to rest.

There may be some truth to this as bipolar 1 mood swings are so unpredictable that it is not always possible to know what day it is, let alone stick to a routine. It is disturbing when mood swings seem to come out of nowhere, but a regular routine may be able to delay or even prevent this from happening.

After many years of hoping for the best outcome and doing nothing, I finally came up with a routine that works for me. The times I have given here are not exact because I am not good when it comes to regulating my daily habits, but I will share my routine with you as it may be helpful.

My daily routine

8:00am   Get out of bed

Feed my cat

Take my thyroid tablet

Make my coffee

Do check in to see how I am feeling

Physically

Emotionally

Mentally

8.30am   Shower and dress

Check emails, Facebook, and Quora

9.30am   Take my other medications

Have breakfast

10.00am   Do light household chores

Phone a friend

11.00am   Start work on the computer

1.00pm   Break for lunch

Sit in the sun and read

2.00pm   Back to work on the computer

3.00pm   Go to the gym

4.30pm   Meditate

Do relaxation exercise

5.00pm   Watch the news

7.00pm   Make supper

8.00pm   Take medication for restless leg syndrome

Catch up on YouTube videos

Watch Netflix

10.00pm   Take my other medications

Journal

Gratitude journal

Check my Daily Wellness Plan

11.00pm   Go to bed

My daily routine will not be like yours because we undoubtedly live very different lifestyles. What is right for me, may not be right for you, but it will give you some guidance.

Your routine

Now see if you can make a list of all the things you do in a day and see if they fit into a routine. If not, see if you can devise one. It doesn't mean you have to stick to it religiously, but it is good for bipolar to get organized and know what you will be doing next.

Recently, I was looking over some old journals and realized how very ill I was with bipolar 1 for many years. It was quite a shock to me as I feel so well now. I also realized why I had been so ill, which was amazing. The truth is I lived in utter chaos for most of my life. I had no idea whether I was coming or going. If this is you, listen up.

In order to put an end to this chaos, I finally got a routine in place and never looked back. Now I know what I should be doing at any time of the day and it has helped me no end. I may not do everything on my routine as I do still have problems with that, but it has helped me enormously.

I wonder if this might apply to you, and if you could start working on a routine which might help you. I do hope this explanation has been of some use to you and you will soon leave the chaotic lifestyle behind.

Schedules are quite different. You schedule appointments to see doctors, to go to the hairdresser, to meet someone for lunch and write those down in your schedule book or planner. If you always remember to write these things down with the name of the person you are meeting, where you are meeting them, and their phone number you will be very organized.

Chapter 35
Triggers

You will no doubt be aware that some things trigger you into having bipolar 1 episodes while others do not. Most people with bipolar 1 have to be vigilant when it comes to everyday life events as they are much more vulnerable than the average person to mood changes. People with bipolar 1 react negatively to life stressors far more often than other people. This can lead to very serious mood swings, often resulting in changes in medication or hospitalization.

It is the rare person that doesn't have triggers. Everybody does to a certain extent. But, unlike the everyday person who feels up or down for a couple of days, when you have bipolar 1 you have to pay attention.

We have to remember that triggers can lead to bipolar 1 mood episodes, but they can often come out of nowhere. You need to be aware that this can happen even when in remission.

Here is a list of a few things that are known to trigger mood changes:

Not enough sleep

As you know by now, it is critical to have good sleep hygiene when you are dealing with bipolar 1. This can take a long time to achieve, with much trial and error, but if you can maintain a good sleep pattern you will be less likely to react badly to negative life events.

It makes sense that when you are worried about something, it is a trigger for a bad night's sleep as you often lie awake for hours. If this is allowed to continue for too long, you are highly likely to experience a manic or hypomanic episode. People also experience depressive episodes with insomnia.

Seasonal events

It was thought that people with unipolar depression experienced more seasonal mood swings, but this has been found not to be the case. Many people with bipolar are susceptible to mood changes in the various seasons. Therefore, it is important to get a good night's sleep in the spring and summer when you are more likely to have a manic or hypomanic reaction.

Also, the winter months can be detrimental to your health and cause a depressive reaction, so if you are sensitive to these changes, be sure to prepare for them by seeing your doctor before the winter months bring darker days.

You might need to use a light box or take vitamin D supplements in the winter when there are fewer daylight hours. These things have proven very helpful for a lot of people with bipolar 1.

Also, remember to stick to your routine. When you have bipolar, you have to do a lot of different things to stay well.

Negative Life Events

There are many stressful things to put up with in life, and each can be detrimental if you have bipolar 1. But certain things have a greater impact on your mood than others.

These are the stressful life events like the loss of someone you love, the loss of a job, financial difficulties, and interpersonal conflict. All these things can make you very sick. With this in mind, it is wise to be in a therapeutic relationship where a therapist can help you cope. It is also good if you have people you can depend upon to help you, but I do know that support is often hard to come by when you have an illness like ours.

Be proactive, make a plan. If you see that something stressful is on the horizon, talk it over with your doctor, therapist, or support person.

Drug and alcohol use

Many medications say you should limit or even abstain from alcohol or drugs altogether in order for them to work properly. If you don't heed this advice, you can be sure you will be unwell. Alcohol in particular is a depressant and can make you depressed. Street drugs can have the opposite effect and bring on a manic episode.

Reproductive cycle

We have discussed menopause in detail in a previous chapter so I won't discuss that here, but there are other times in a woman's life where she finds that mood cycles can spring from any event.

If you are pregnant, or trying to become pregnant, you should be wary of mood changes as many women have problems at these times. 20% of women have mania leading to psychosis during pregnancy or during the post-partum period.

Be sure to talk to your doctor before getting pregnant because you may require a change in medication. Some medications are contra-indicated in pregnancy so it is important to acclimatize yourself first.

Many women have problems with menstruation, too. Mood cycles are common to most people in menstruation, let alone a person who has mood swings as an illness. Be sure to take extra special care of yourself at this time.

Caffeine

Caffeine is a stimulant that can be a trigger in bipolar 1. Many people are highly sensitive to too much caffeine, and when you have bipolar 1 it can cause a manic reaction, especially if you are not getting enough sleep. It can also interfere with your medications, so do cut down if you can.

Good stress

That seems to be a contradiction in terms, I know, but there is evidence that positive events can also bring on mood changes in bipolar 1. If you win a lot of money, get a promotion, fall in love, or have a baby, this can lead to a mood episode. Many women have mood events after they have a baby, as we know, but men who are new fathers can also have this effect if they have bipolar 1.

Every day triggers

These are all general things that can trigger bipolar 1 mood swings, but it pays to recognize your everyday triggers as well. There is no doubt that we are all triggered by these major life events, but it is the little things that could go unnoticed that can cause a lot of problems, too.

I have a list of triggers in my Daily Wellness Plan and shall share a few of them with you. These are the things that I have to watch out for all the time in order to stay well:

- Feeling rushed
- Doing too much
- Losing things
- Financial problems
- Being over-tired
- Robo calls

Now that I am aware of these triggers, I can do something about them to prevent any problems that might ensue.

Feeling rushed

I feel rushed when I haven't left enough time for a task or event. This often applies when I have an appointment and have to be across town in fifteen minutes. Now, instead of leaving it to the last minute, I leave ten minutes early, take a good book, and read it if I have to wait.

I also used to get tired and irritable, so I now make sure I don't make any more than three appointments in one day. I may have chores and errands to run all over town, but now instead of doing them all in one day, I divide them up and do them over a two-day period.

Also, I am definitely not a morning person, so never make appointments in the morning if I can help it. You may have a specific time of day when you are at your best, so be sure to use that time wisely.

Many people feel rushed when they have bipolar 1. It is quite normal when you take on too much, and especially when you are not feeling well. It is best to remind yourself that you can do things the next day. Not everything has to be done right now.

Doing too much

I don't know why it is, but I always used to think I should be doing more than I was actually doing and this resulted in a low mood, and even depression if I wasn't careful.

Because of this, I have limited what I do in the house as well. I may have a lot of housework, laundry, and cooking to do, but decide I just can't do it in one day like other people, so I divide it up over a few days so as not to feel overloaded.

Take the time to ask yourself if you are doing too much. Of course, you may have a lot of responsibilities which are insurmountable. In that case, do carve out fifteen minutes of your day to rest and relax. Do a body scan and see where you have tension. Do muscle relaxation exercises before returning to your usual tasks. You may be good at meditating by now, so take time out to do that.

Losing things

I was famous for losing things. You may be as well. It is so easy to lay down your keys on the table, for example, then forget where you have left them when you need them. This can be a big trigger for a mood change.

Now I make sure I have a place for everything, so that I always know where to find things. In the case of my keys, I have a hook beside the door I use most frequently so I can always find them there.

Another rule I have is not to put things down, but put them away. It is a simple rule but keeps the house tidy and you can always find the things you are looking for.

I am a bit of a perfectionist, so take this maybe too far, but I have all my closets color coded so I can find my clothes quickly, and I keep all my drawers and cupboards in order.

I am not saying you need a touch of OCD, but it is good to find a suitable place to keep things so you can always find them.

Financial problems

This is a hard one, as situations fluctuate all the time. But, now instead of forgetting what money I have in the bank, I check my balance daily online. That way I know whether I can spend a certain amount or not.

I do try to stick to a budget as well which helps keep me on track. I pay all my bills online and they are taken out as soon as my check is deposited so I never have to worry that I won't have enough money left to pay a bill.

I also pay myself first. This is a habit I got into a long time ago and it has proved invaluable. Instead of waiting to see if I have anything left over to save at the end of the month, I pay myself first, then it is all done.

I only have two credit cards so I can keep up with that. I have a normal, everyday card, and a business card on which I keep a running balance.

You have to simplify your life when you have bipolar 1 or you will get into all kinds of trouble. Do work on a budget and see where you can cut back on your expenses. You can find many helpful websites on this subject.

Being overtired

I find it very easy to get overtired because I don't like going to bed.

If I sit up after 11, I am in trouble. I can't get to sleep, for one thing, then feel draggy the next day. This could often spark off a depressive episode if I left it for a few nights, so I now make sure I am in bed before 11 every night.

It is just a case of being firm with myself and knowing that going to bed early is for my own good. I know some people would think 11 o'clock at night is late, but it is early for me.

What time do you go to bed? Are you able to stick to a routine? Feeling worn out is certainly a trigger for bipolar 1. Make a bed time and stick to it. Don't sit up when you are tired. Go to bed.

Robo calls

Finally, the dreaded robo calls. You must know all about them. They are the things anger is made of, and that is definitely not good for bipolar 1 mood swings.

These days, I don't waste time on them at all. When the phone rings, I check the caller ID, and if I don't know them, I don't answer the phone.

I do hope this is of some use to you. I encourage you to write a list of your particular triggers and keep it in your Daily Wellness Plan binder. Then you are more likely to avoid them. Avoidance is key if you want to stay well.

Chapter 36
Coping skills

You have probably heard that term before when it comes to being in control of bipolar 1. But if you are anything like I was, you don't really know what coping skills are. I didn't know this for a long time, to my detriment, as I had nothing to fall back on when I became ill.

However, coping skills are not meant to be for when things go wrong. They are for when things are going right, too, so that you can be prepared for things that might go wrong in the future.

Unfortunately, with bipolar 1, you can never really rest. Instead, you have to be forever vigilant. It is like waiting for the other shoe to drop. If you are not vigilant all the time, you are likely to be surprised by another mood swing. Bipolar 1 never goes away.

It certainly seems unfair, doesn't it, when most of the world's population doesn't have to worry about being ill all the time, but bipolar 1 makes it impossible to get complacent and think that everything will be fine later on?

I have been well for a few years now. This makes me very happy, but I know I can't forget that I do actually have bipolar even when it seems like I don't. It is the beast that lurks around the corner just waiting to catch you out when you least expect it. It just lies in wait for an opportunity to pounce.

This is why you need to be thinking about using coping skills all the time. You need to have a lot of tricks up your sleeve to outwit this beast. If you are not accustomed to using coping skills, it is time to get started. That, and your Daily Wellness Plan will save you from the bipolar 1 monster. If you can pay attention to your triggers all the better.

It is a tall order for us folk. Yet, when we can say we are coping well with our disorder, we will be better than the next person who is always well and doesn't have to worry about being sick.

Time to learn coping skills.

I thought the best way to talk about coping skills would be to share the ones I use that are in my Daily Wellness Plan under **THINGS TO DO EVERY DAY**. They are many and varied, and in fact, I could go on listing them forever, but that would only confuse both of us in the end. Some we have already discussed, and others we will cover later.

Here are just a few of my coping skills. I hope this will give you incentive to write a list of your own.

- Go to bed and get up at the same time every day
- Stick to your morning routine
- Take your medication
- Eat a nutritious diet
- Eat at regular mealtimes
- Write in your Gratitude journal
- Journal
- Check in with how you are feeling today
  - Physically
  - Mentally
  - Emotionally
- Connect with others
- Sit in the sun for 15 minutes every day
- Drink plenty of water
- Relax and do meditation
- Do something creative
- Exercise
- Do something for fun

By the way, I believe in journaling as writing in a journal helps you deal with your emotional struggles. It is a safe place to be you. You don't need to write neatly, or even spell properly. You can just write streams of consciousness and nobody minds at all.

I always buy attractive journals. I don't use a school note book or pieces of paper that get lost. I like a beautiful journal with a really creative cover. You can buy amazing journals online. I also write with a nice Sharpie pen. I hate scratchy pens, or pens that blob or run out in the middle of a word.

I am also big on Gratitude. If you are grateful for things, I find you really appreciate your life. I am grateful for all kinds of things like the fact that I have a roof over my head, I have a reliable car in the garage, and I can breathe. Without breath you are not likely to survive for long, so I am grateful for every breath I take.

You will be grateful for other things, too, so a Gratitude journal is the way to go. You can also get some beautiful ones online. Start by thinking of three things you are grateful for. Add to your list every day.

Your coping skills

See if you can write a list of coping skills you can do every day to better cope with your bipolar 1. If you think about it, I am sure you will have quite a list of things to refer to when you feel another bipolar 1 mood swing is on the horizon. Don't forget to file your list in your Daily Wellness Plan.

Chapter 37
Mood charts

Mood charts are just what they say they are. They make sense of your moods because you can see all the information in one view, and they are very useful in keeping a record of your mood swings. If you are a visual person, mood charts are for you.

I kept a mood chart for many years, but when I couldn't find one that suited me, I had to draw one up myself. I wrote all my symptoms down because half of them weren't covered in any ready-made mood chart. There is very little room for everything in any case.

I included depression, mania, psychosis, anxiety, panic, and pain, my usual list that I keep in my Daily Wellness Plan. I also added things like medication, weight, and sleep.

This was a long time ago, and I see that mood charts have improved somewhat over the years. They now list things like:

- A mood scale with severity of moods 1 to 10
- Hours of sleep
- Medications taken
- Side effects
- Substance abuse

- Weight
- Anxiety
- Irritability

You can find any number of mood charts on line. DBSA (Depression and Bipolar Support Alliance) has a whole array of them that you might find useful. Or if you prefer, you can use a mood chart app on your phone.

Making a mood chart

However, you might be like me and want to use your individual mood chart. It is not easy to find a comprehensive chart, so a custom one is often the way to go. I recommend you use a sheet of graph paper and draw your chart using a ruler. Don't forget to make photocopies of an empty chart or you won't have a blank one when you have filled in your first chart. File your mood charts in your Daily Wellness Plan binder.

One good thing about mood charts is you can take them to your next doctor's appointment where you can discuss your moods in detail, and also make a note of any problems you may be having with your medication. Most doctors are pleased when you take the initiative, so it is always worthwhile doing them.

I know you can make a good job of doing mood charts, and this will help you get well because it is easy to see when a mood swing is on the way. Do what you can to track your moods.

Chapter 38
Support system

If you read other books and articles, you will find they always say a good support system is 'essential' if you want to live well with bipolar, but what they don't understand is that it is not always possible to find a good support system. It is desirable, yes, but not always easy to achieve.

However, you might be one of the lucky few who have relatives and friends who have stuck by you throughout the course of your illness.

I am sure you will have noticed by now that many people disappear from your life when you have bipolar 1. It is a relationship wrecker. No two ways about it.

This particularly applies in mania. As you probably know by now, if you have a manic episode, you are very likely to say and do things that other people do not approve of. Your head is bursting with ideas, people move far too slowly for your liking, and they basically get on your nerves. So, what do you do? Wreck another relationship.

This is bad news if you want to find people for a support group!

I have had much experience with this in the past because I have almost come to blows with many different people. I couldn't keep relationships with friends or relatives at all.

I have few original people in my life these days, but have learned to live without the ones that have gone. Luckily, new people have come along, and now that I am well, I am more able to keep the relationships going.

A support system is nice to have

Nevertheless, a support system, if not a must, is nice to have when things go wrong. And they will do with bipolar 1, as you must know. It is also good to have some people in your corner when things are going right so that you can prepare them for the worst. But all these things are hard to orchestrate.

I never had a support system at all for most of my life. As I say, relatives and friends simply disappeared, and husbands didn't want to know. Eventually, when I came to America, I was so sick that I had to use a local clinic to manage my bipolar. There I found many people to fill the gaps in my support system. I also joined several peer support groups which were very helpful indeed.

If you have a local clinic, you are very fortunate as you can usually lean on them for support when you need it. Make the most of it. Join support groups. Make your needs heard.

One thing you have to learn when you have bipolar 1 is to advocate for yourself. No matter how seriously ill you are, if you don't advocate for yourself, you will never get what you want.

I now have a very wide support network, but not the

people you would expect. I do hope you have some reliable people in your life. That would be a huge bonus if you do.

. Here is a list of the people who are now supportive of me:

- Family doctor
- Nurse practitioner
  (there is no psychiatrist in this town)
- Nurse (at the clinic)
- Case worker (at the clinic)
- Peer support manager (at the clinic)
- Psychotherapist (private)
- Pharmacist
- Brother
- Niece
- Nephew
- Cousin
- Friend
- Dentist
- Pen friends
- Bank manager
- Bank manager's assistant

Yes, it is rather a motley crew, but I do have some extraordinary people on my side. Whether, or not, I can discuss my problems with them remains to be seen.
I tend to keep things to myself.

Once when I came out of the hospital I was told to go to the bank and let them do my statement every month because the thought of that filled me with dread. I thought this was not possible, but it was. I told my bank manager and her assistant that I had bipolar 1 and educated them on it because I thought they might help me when I needed it. Since that time, they have always asked me how I am getting on, and showed a great interest in my illness. They also looked after my credit cards when I had manic episodes.

My dentist is also very helpful and always asks how I am. You just never know who might be supportive if you need them.

Support groups

I hope you will take advantage of any support groups in your area. You can get a lot of questions answered at these groups, and there will be people who are suffering like you, so they are able to empathize. Do check out online groups, as well, as they can be very helpful. You can make friends on there with people like you who are trying to live successfully with bipolar 1.

You should know that there are also groups for members of your family should they need support. Many parents and partners go to these groups, then they don't feel so alone with their challenges. NAMI (National Alliance on Mental Illness) does lectures and courses for relatives and friends. These are very helpful.

Your Support System

I hope you will make a list of all your supporters. Think very carefully, and don't forget to ask them before you put them down on the list.

Chapter 39
Relationships

Let me say again, there is no doubt about it bipolar 1 is a relationship killer. When you are manic it is like swinging a wrecking ball at those you love and care about the most.

No holds are barred in mania. It is sometimes impossible to keep your mouth shut – let alone all the weird things you get up to that will seriously damage relationships with the people you love, even people who have been support-ive of you throughout your illness.

It is very unfair indeed that you are sick and have to watch how you conduct yourself when you are manic. What other illness causes people to worry about changing their whole personality? I can't think of any.

They say diabetes is comparable to bipolar, in so much as they have to take medication or insulin every day. But their personality doesn't change periodically, and they don't have to worry about ruining every relationship they cherish if they forget to take their medication. And, as you know, even when you do take your medication, that is not a watertight guarantee that you can keep bipolar 1 symptoms at bay.

Relationships when you are manic

If you are like me, you will have a whole string of broken relationships in your wake. People you once knew will have nothing to do with you, they will even cross the street in order to avoid saying, *"Hi!"*

When you are manic, arguments and angry comments ensue. It is just a matter of time before you lose your mind and say something that will hurt or offend another person. And then what happens? They stop speaking to you altogether, and cut themselves out of your life. It is so disheartening.

The real problem comes when they will not accept your apology. I have tried apologizing for the dreadful things I have said, many times, and been rejected by even the most faithful friends.

Once I really offended a friend and wrote a long letter of apology to her. Did this make any difference? No. She just blocked me from her life. And I thought she would have understood because she had a brother who had schizo-phrenia. But sometimes, apologies are just not enough, apparently. They want you to be a different person, like you were when you were well.

How many times have you embarrassed people by being obnoxious when manic? It is tempting to talk loudly, to interrupt, and to insist people listen to you. But soon enough you will be labeled a bore and not someone people want to mix with.

And how about the flirting? Don't tell me you don't flirt when manic because I won't believe you. Flirting is one thing, that is relatively harmless, but when it comes to jumping into bed with complete strangers, that is another matter entirely. Your near perfect marriage is suddenly dead and you are getting divorce papers in the mail.

Partners just do not understand bipolar. No matter how hard they try, and some really do try, it is almost impossible for them to understand what is happening in your mind when you have sex with people you don't know and don't even feel guilty right afterwards. You will soon feel guilty when you are well.

The real danger lies in the effects of all these casual sexual exploits. What happens when you get an STD? And heaven forbid, when you get pregnant.

And your partner really won't understand when you wipe out the savings, spending freely at the casino, or investing in some tricky business deal.

That is when it becomes too much. Even relationships without bipolar fail over financial issues, let alone a relationship where one partner thinks nothing of wiping out your savings. People never take kindly to bankruptcies and that is what happens to a lot of people who have reckless manias.

Relationships when you are depressed

I haven't forgotten how hard it is to conduct any relationship when you are depressed, either. That is another thing entirely. Partners, parents, siblings, friends, nobody understands why you just cannot get out of bed and take a shower in the morning. It is beyond their comprehension.

It is hard to understand why your partner sits in a chair all day staring at the floor. Why can't they just snap out of it? Why don't they see it is ruining your relationship?

Maybe your partner is helpful, at first, but even the most supportive person often breaks down and admits they can't cope with your depression. It is true that care takers have a very high risk of getting sick themselves, and you can't have two seriously depressed people in one house.

What can you do?

So, what can you do with all these relationships that are hanging on by a thread? The best thing to try is educating people. I am not saying this is easy – sometimes you go to a lot of trouble to find just the right article on the internet, you print it out and hand it to your partner or your parent, but you just can't make them read it, let alone understand it. You can hardly understand bipolar 1 yourself half the time, can you?

Some family members will never try to improve their knowledge about bipolar 1, even though it could be useful to them. They are just not readers, are too angry with you, or are just not interested. What can you do with relationships like this that are often doomed from the start?

Bipolar families

I haven't had a family for a long time, so I am not much use in advising you on this one. I have one brother left who lives in Australia so I never see him at all. We write emails and make phone calls, but that is it. I have, however, found some relatives on Facebook quite recently, but none of them live in this country.

You, on the other hand, almost certainly have a family. You may still be in touch with them, or bipolar may have caused irreparable damage. After all, we are closest to our families, so when we are just being our bipolar self, we can do a lot of harm to our relationships.

Of course, you will encounter problems with families no matter what you try to do because people in general do not understand bipolar or even want to understand it. And parents may well be upset because they might think that you have bipolar disorder because of them, and they feel guilty.

Many people do acquire bipolar disorder because their parents have some kind of mental illness. That is a fact. So, it must be difficult to actually acknowledge that you have passed a serious illness on to your children.

Friends

Friends, even those you have had since first grade, can suddenly disappear out of your life when they get the news that you have bipolar disorder. This is not because they don't like you, it is nearly always because they are afraid that they might catch it (yes!), or they don't understand it. When you have people like this in your life find a suitable article online and give it to them to read. But as I have said, don't expect them to read it, let alone understand it.

If you are very lucky, you will have true friends who stand by and support you when times get tough. You are the exception to the rule, believe me. But good for you when this happens. We could all do with people to support us. That is a fact.

You may be one of those people who can't even make friends or keep them. I seem to think this is very common when you have bipolar 1. People just do not understand this illness, and can't understand you either. One day you are on top of the world, then the next you are suicidal. Who could possibly understand that?

So don't be too hard on other people. They have their own lives to live, and it often doesn't include you. It is unfair that we have to be ashamed of having bipolar as no other illness requires such humility.

Bipolar marriages

Bipolar and marriage just don't seem to go together. I have been married three times and could never get it right. I am thankfully living alone now, so only have myself to put up with. The fact is that 90% of marriages fail when one partner has bipolar disorder. It is a sobering thought, isn't it?

I know a very loving couple, at least they were, who have weathered all kinds of bipolar storms. The wife has extreme bipolar 1 mood swings with psychosis where she loses all her inhibitions and makes scathing remarks towards her husband. But I didn't worry. I thought they were managing so well. Then, out of the blue, he wrote to me and said she had left and he never wants to see or hear from her again! So much for happy marriages.

It is a very sad state of affairs when marriages are doomed before they even begin. But that is the nature of this illness. If you can't educate your partner, you just hope they have the patience of Job.

Having children

Then there are the children. Personally, I do not have any children, for which I am thankful. I am quite sure I would have ruined their lives otherwise. But if you have children, I should think you have your work cut out for you.

I have read a great deal about how people with bipolar 1 have shouted at their children for the least little thing. And I have also read that parents can be violent towards their children when in a dysphoric mania, then their behavior really crosses the line.

I wonder how many of you are reluctant to even have children if you know that people with bipolar disorder run a very high-risk of having children that will inherit it at some stage in their lives. It must be very difficult to cope with that.

Getting it right

The only thing I have found helpful is to learn to accept that this is what is going to happen if you have bipolar 1. Really. I know that sounds defeatist, but it is the truth. If you can't change it, then expect things to go wrong.

I am lucky to live alone. And now that I am well, I no longer worry about manic or depressive episodes, or hurting other people.

I send emails to my brother in Australia most weeks. When I was in one of my bipolar episodes, I used to send terrible letters to him, accusing him of many things. Finally, he suggested something that has worked to this day. He told me not to press SEND, but to put my letter in the DRAFT folder instead. This could work for you, too, and save some of your relationships.

Of course, the one thing you can do, and hopefully get right, is to find a medication cocktail which will keep your bipolar 1 in check. I know this is often a very tall order. It takes time, and the side effects can be bad. But if you are able to find something that helps, you are on your way to better relationships.

Fortunately, after a lifetime of medication trials, I have found an anti-psychotic that works for me. I call it my magic pill. I cannot recommend it to you, however, as medication is a unique journey. What suits me may well cause you problems. Nobody knows.

If all else fails, do get therapy. That can be very helpful indeed for coping with relationship problems.

When should you tell?

This is the age-old question. I have very mixed feelings about this and many people disagree with me, but I have found it best to keep my diagnosis to myself. Now, that is impossible, of course, because I have written two books on the subject. But overall, I still think it is better to only share your diagnosis with people who have to know, like your partner and possibly your parents. But even sharing your diagnosis with parents is a gamble. Before you know it, the rest of the family will know.

I wouldn't advise telling your whole family, your boss, your colleagues, your friends, or even strangers you meet in the street. People just do not understand bipolar disorder and will not want to know you after you disclose your diagnosis.

I had to leave a church after telling someone I had bipolar disorder as people got up, with an excuse, when I sat down next to them. I felt like a leper. Every Sunday was a trial as people always avoided me, and little groups dispersed the minute I joined them.

So, it is up to you. Some people have been very successful about sharing their diagnosis, and others don't see any reason to hide it or perpetuate the stigma. But overall, I am still of the opinion that it should only be shared with people that need to know.

Of course, if you are seeing somebody and thinking of going steady, I would advise you to tell them before you get too involved. However, I don't believe you should tell somebody on the first date. They will probably reject you and tell all their friends that you have bipolar.

To tell, or not to tell, is a debatable topic, and everybody has had their own experiences. I can only tell you how I have managed it, and leave it up to you if you want to share this information with others.

Chapter 40
Work, school, and money

Work

I am sure most people with bipolar 1 have problems with work, school, or money. They just go together, and make you sick. It is very hard to make a job work for you if you have bipolar 1, school is perhaps even worse, and money problems plague us all.

Work is something we nearly all have to do in order to live, but when you have bipolar 1 it is often a difficult thing to get right. The one common denominator seems to be that most people with such a serious diagnosis as bipolar 1 have such a hard time sticking to a job that they are a miserable failure at a working life.

I have had innumerable jobs in my lifetime, all of which were ruined by my bipolar 1 behavior. I have had jobs that are hard to come by, but are even harder to maintain. And I have tried to cope with the stress and strain in vain.

I have had two jobs as marketing manager for large companies, both hospitals, as a matter of fact, which I am familiar with because I am an R.N. (Registered Nurse). Unfortunately, I couldn't keep either of these jobs, even though the money was very good and I had a company car as incentives. When you are sick with bipolar 1 you will have a hard time keeping any job, and that is for sure.

I lost the two marketing jobs due to depression. One day, I walked into the office at one of these jobs, sat down at my desk and cried. I had nothing to cry about, but I just couldn't take another day of it, so I packed my bag and left.

Other times, I couldn't attend board meetings because I had far too much anxiety. Nobody understood that, so I had to make up all kinds of excuses to satisfy their curiosity as to why I couldn't join them in the board room.

However, I did manage to stick to my nursing job for eleven years and would probably still be there if I was younger and had stayed in England. So, I have to reassure you and tell you that it is possible to get well enough with bipolar 1 to allow you to make a success of a career.

At the time, I was on the perfect medication cocktail which was the answer. If you are lucky enough to have found the right medications for you, then you will no doubt be able to hold down the job of your choosing.

Unfortunately, I became menopausal shortly after arriving in America, as I have said, so all my trusty medicines were of no use at all.

My answer to you, if you are not able to further your career, is to stop thinking big and decide to do something less challenging. Bipolar 1 brains think they like a challenge, but they soon realize they do not. It is best to start off by doing something you enjoy, and are good at, that won't tax you altogether.

Even part time work is better than nothing. Try part time work and see if you enjoy that. You might be able to hold down a job then without being fired from every full-time position you fail at. When you have mania and depression, not to mention anxiety, you are better able to manage to work part time. There is no doubt about it.

However, I have heard some people who are very high functioning say they have made a very successful career even with bipolar 1, and I admire them.

School/college/university

This illness is peculiar in that it starts just when you are thinking of bettering your education. Everybody has high hopes for you when you are eighteen and doing well in school, only to find that you cannot manage to progress to university or college. Or if you are lucky enough to start a college degree, you may have to leave due to your illness.

Bipolar disorder has a very bad habit of appearing in the late teens, early twenties, just when you are about to make a go of your life. It is dreadful – it is unfair – but that is the way it is. I have always found that the saying, *"Life is unfair,"* has explained a lot of things to me when trying to cope with bipolar 1.

But do what you can to work on this, even though it is hard, as education really matters in this society. You are lost without it. Do try to get an early diagnosis, and get a second opinion if necessary.

I have to congratulate people who have done well at university as I know how hard it is to concentrate. Nevertheless, there are many people who are doing very responsible jobs now because they persevered with their education.

Staying well on medication

Only when you have a correct diagnosis can you expect to stay well on the medication that has been prescribed for you. Medication is such an individual thing, and it takes a lot of trial and error to get it right, but when you do, it can help you enormously. It has certainly helped me. It has been a life-saver.

Personally, I didn't do well in school for many reasons. Both my parents died before I was fifteen, so I had to basically fend for myself. This didn't leave much room for a fulfilling education, but I caught up later, when I felt better, and did my nursing degree. So, it can be done.

One thing that will let you down if you are attending college or university is that you will be tempted to live the way of your peers, and that is doomed to failure with bipolar 1.

Drinking alcohol to excess, taking drugs, even staying up late night after night is detrimental to bipolar 1 mania and depression. If you indulge in these things, your studies are almost doomed to failure from the start. Yet I know it takes a lot of will power to remain an outsider when it comes to partying. It is a horrible choice, but one you need to work on if you want to make a success of your life.

Money

I am not an accountant, and I don't work in a bank, but I have managed to get my affairs in order so that I usually spend within my means, and that is what you need to do if you want to remain well.

Mania has a terrible influence on your budget. There is no doubt about that. No matter how much you earn, if you are not careful with your finances, you will be sorry as things can get out of hand very quickly.

If you do not budget already, learn how to do it. There are innumerable articles online that you can read. There is also a glut of You Tube videos you can watch on the subject. Learning to budget is the only way to go. You will not be sorry once you get it right.

I realize that bipolar 1 mania makes you want to spend, I was the world's worst when it came to spending, but somehow or other you need to refrain from getting into debt.

Personally, after one manic episode where I bought three cars in one week, I started leaving my credit cards at the bank the minute I started feeling a little off. It was always a joke at the bank because the manager said they daren't look out of the window when I was coming for fear they wouldn't recognize the car in the car park.

Yes, mania can make you do the most stupid things, things you will surely regret later. I know how wonderful it is to shop. And if you are like me, there is nothing better than seeing a whole array of boxes from Amazon piled up on the doorstep. What fun it is to open them all, it is like Christmas every day. But then you notice that there are duplicates, and even triplicates, of things you once thought you might like and now realize you no longer need, so back they go when the mania has run its course. It is a Godsend that Amazon takes returns!

You may be having a great deal of difficulty staying in a job, so the money will be tight. You might qualify for social security if you are lucky. You will need to look up the rules as I don't know exactly what you need to do these days, but do know that bipolar disorder is one of the illnesses that qualify for monthly SSDI.

But never think you can rely on social security as the pay is very low indeed. It is barely possible to exist on social security, so if you can manage it, you will need to hold down some kind of work if only part time.

Chapter 41
When things break down

Unfortunately, with the best will in the world, you are likely to get sick with bipolar 1. You may be taking your medications at the right time each day, doing all the things I have enumerated in previous chapters, but even so, you just cannot cope with the many mood episodes you are being forced to endure.

If you are not taking your medications, you can be sure to have mood episodes. If they don't come immediately, while you are on your "med holiday," they will come soon after when the medications have left your system.

Either way, you can get pretty sick with bipolar 1.

Depression

I don't know which is worse, mania or depression, but either way they are difficult to cope with. Depression can come out of the blue, for no reason at all, or may follow a manic episode. You have been on top of the world for a couple of weeks, then boom, you are in a deep depression where the only answer seems to be to kill yourself.

Of course, this is no answer to the problem as the symptoms are only temporary, but it can seem feasible when you are in the depths of despair. Depression sucks the life out of you. It leaves you wanting. The only way to cope with the beast is to treat yourself kindly and take your medication. Self-care is everything when it comes to bipolar 1.

As you well know, depression can take a turn for the worse very quickly, and then it is a real danger to your wellbeing. You may have to stay in bed because you have no energy for anything else. If you have an understanding partner or parent you will be better off than someone who lives alone, but even partners and parents find it difficult to cope with you when you are severely depressed.

And suicidal ideation cannot be ignored. If you are suicidal, you will need all the help you can get, and being under twenty-four-hour watch in a hospital bed may be a life saver.

After a week, or so, of being in the depths of despair, there is no getting round it, you will need to be admitted to the hospital. We shall discuss this further in the following chapter.

Mania

If you do not get well spontaneously on your own, the outcome is usually the same with mania. Many people have been hospitalized in mania, and they have done well under supervision with the right medication.

But you could have done a great deal of damage whilst in your manic episode, and you may be so far gone as to not recognize that you are sick. If people try to tell you that you need to go to the hospital, it will be a shock to you when you feel so well.

It is very difficult to convince a person in mania that they need extra care, yet mania is so destructive you have to go to the hospital for your own and other people's welfare. This applies especially if you are homicidal. Sad events have taken place in a bipolar 1 manic rage.

Psychosis

If, unfortunately, you have a psychotic episode, with either severe depression or severe mania, you will also need to be taken to the hospital. You may be able to manage well on your own for a few days, but psychosis usually gets worse and you will need more care than your family is able to give you. People do not understand psychosis, so you need professional help. And the best place to get that is in the hospital.

There is no shame in being admitted to the hospital. Many people with bipolar 1 have been there before you. It is a difficult disease to manage on your own, so a little help is a wonderful thing. Also, getting the right medication is a huge bonus.

Chapter 42
Crisis plan

The best thing you can do is to make a crisis plan when you are well. When you are sick, you are unable to make good decisions for yourself and can easily end up being in a worse situation than before. Make a crisis plan and file it in your Daily Wellness Plan binder where you or your supporters can find it. Or you can make copies and give them to them.

Hopefully, you will have someone there to help you when you get sick. I never did, and had to rely on my crisis plan for assistance.

In order to write a good crisis plan, you will need to do a little towards it when you think of things that matter to you. Don't try to do it all in one sitting, or you will undoubtedly leave things out.

It is important to let your supporters know where you keep your plan so they can go to it if necessary. I hope it won't be necessary, of course, but it is far better to be safe than sorry.

You want to make it as easy as possible for them to help you should the time come. It is very scary for supporters to suddenly have to deal with a bipolar crisis. If you have a plan already in place, it will ease their burden.

Here are a few things you can work on when you are devising your crisis plan:

- Make a list of all your supporters, their addresses and phone numbers.

- You may want them to do different things for you, so it would be a good idea to make this clear on your plan. Be sure to discuss it with them first. If someone could look after your children while you are sick then ask them if they would do that for you and assign them that job.

- Maybe you have pets, so that would be something you would need to sort out before you get sick. Make arrangements for them, so you are not worrying about them when you are in the hospital.

- When I was in the hospital, I used to always have the problem of paying the bills as I had nobody to do it for me. Whether you are in the hospital, or not, the bills will come rolling in, and if you are not there to pay them you could get your electricity or water cut off.

- Be sure to think ahead about financial matters. I decided to let the bank pay my bills out of my income as soon as I got paid. They can easily make these arrangements for you, and it puts your mind at ease. Make friends with people at the bank and tell them that you may sometimes have to go to the hospital and will need their help to take care of your finances. I am sure most banks will be happy to help you with this.

- Don't forget to make a list of the medical people who can help you. List your family doctor, your psychiatrist, your therapist, and your pharmacist along with their phone numbers. Also, if you have a clinic in your area, list the people there who would be willing to help.

- Make a list of all the medications you are taking. The names, the dosages, and the time of day you take them. Also, list what you take them for.

- Now, very important, you need to make sure to list the medications that have given you bad side effects, as when you go to the hospital the doctors usually change your medications. If you have had adverse effects from a particular medication, it is better that they know about it in advance.

- You may have had experiences with hospitals before, for good and bad, so you will want to make a list of all the hospitals that are acceptable and those that aren't. When you are depressed or manic, you can easily be sent to a hospital that is not of your choosing, but if you make a list beforehand, your supporters will be able to make your wishes known.

- Also, state any treatments that are unacceptable to you, like ECT, if that is something you would not want for yourself. You might also request that you not be put in restraints or isolation and hope they take your request into account. I have a tremendous fear of being put in restraints and isolated away from other people. Luckily, this has never been a problem, but it is in my crisis plan, just in case.

- If you want this to be a legal document, you can get an Advance Directive and get one of your supporters to sign it. That could be quite expensive, but it may be worth it for your peace of mind.

Chapter 43
Hospital

We have already mentioned going into the hospital if you are severely ill or suicidal. It is not something many people like to do, but may actually save your life.

I have been in the hospital in England and America more times than I could possibly remember and have to say it is not my favorite place to visit. But, when necessary, it has been there which is very reassuring if I am very sick.

If you have been in a psychiatric hospital, you will have many tales to tell. Some people tell me they had good experiences, especially in the UK, but I can't say I would agree with them.

In fact, I have a long list of all the things I don't like about these hospitals, including the food, and have consulted it on occasion when I get the idea into my head that I should go. I keep the list on my fridge door to remind myself that I really hate it in the hospital!

However, a stay in a hospital may be just what you need, and you might have a nice hospital in your vicinity. If that is the case, do write the name of it down on your crisis plan and put it in your Daily Wellness Plan binder.

I have not known a hospital that will take you in without a referral. In my case, I always ended up in the ER if I was very sick, and a member of the clinic staff would come to admit me to the hospital.

If I was that sick, I didn't have a say in it, and was usually kept under involuntary status for ten days to two weeks, and sometimes a whole month. If I was suicidal, which I have been more than once, I was kept under 24/7 supervision for at least the next forty-eight hours.

I have been to many hospitals and they all seem to be run the same way when it comes to admission. When you are admitted, they give you a book on the hospital rules to read and, if you are well enough to read it, you will find out their policies on medications and other practices. It is always a bit uncertain as to whether you can refuse certain medications, or not, as it varies from location to location. It seems that in my local hospital, you don't have a say in the matter. You would need to check on that.

When you are admitted, you generally have a visit from the psychiatrist who will take a note of your history and any medications you may be on. This is where your crisis plan comes in handy. If you are admitted when you are not too sick, do take your plan with you so that you can give it to the doctor on duty. This will list all your medications which will be of great help to the medical staff.

If I have been very depressed, I am usually allowed to sleep for a couple of days, but after that, I am encouraged to mix with the other patients in the unit. Most people in the hospital are sick with schizophrenia, bipolar 1, or drug abuse. People with bipolar 2 do not generally need to go to the hospital as their hypomania can be managed at home.

I do not remember what happened to me during one of my manic episodes, but watching other people in mania, I see that they usually pace up and down and are very loud and unruly. Then they are put on different medication.

You will be able to meet the other patients in your unit in the day room during the break. I cannot tell you what all hospitals do as they are all different when it comes to this policy.

In all the hospitals I have been in they have various activities and psychotherapy sessions. Some have group therapy sessions while others see the patient one-on-one. A hospital I was in had both. I always found these groups helpful, and learned more about my disorder and how to cope with it.

The other activities vary widely from hospital to hospital. You may get exercise routines, arts and crafts, sports like basketball, or even music therapy. It is usually best to attend these sessions as they will be assessing you accordingly, and it could make a difference in how long you stay in.

One thing you will find in most hospitals is that you will not be able to choose what you eat, where you sleep, or the medications you take. All these things will be pre-arranged for everybody on the unit. Of course, it would be impossible to cater to everyone's different tastes, but it is disturbing not to have any choices about what you do with your life.

When you are in the hospital, be sure to write things down like what the doctor has said to you, if you are able. It is difficult to remember what has happened after the event, and you want to make the most of your stay.

Going home

I, and most other people, find it somewhat difficult to adjust to leaving the hospital as the times for everything in the hospital are regimented, and you know exactly what you should be doing at any given hour of the day. This routine is very helpful when you are sick and unable to fend for yourself, but when you get home, it can be difficult to get back into your own routine.

Do take great care of yourself when you return home. Be sure you get enough sleep and rest, and eat a wholesome diet. When you can get back to your exercise routine, do so, as this will help you recover more quickly. Also, remember to take the new medication your doctor has given you in order to stay well.

I hope you never have to go to the hospital, of course, but if you do, you will be more aware of the system by now. The aim is to keep you safe, and that is for the best.

Summing it up

We have covered a lot of different topics in this chapter and have learned about:

- Daily Wellness Plan
- Routine and reminders
- Triggers
- Coping skills
- Mood charts
- Support systems
- Relationships
- Work, school and money
- When things break down
- Crisis plan
- Hospital

If you should have to go to the hospital, be sure to get some help when you come home as this is a very challenging time for you. It is sometimes difficult to remain well without the support of the hospital setting. Be sure to take good care of yourself.

Family

As you can see, it is very difficult to cope with bipolar 1, and all the chaos it brings into your life, but with a little support and encouragement, things can have a good outcome. We want our loved one to live the best life possible, to be able to work, manage their own finances and be successful in life. It can be done.

Also, you will have learned about hospitals and the challenges your loved one will face should they need to go in for treatment. It is not easy being in a mental hospital, not to mention the stigma attached to it. Many people have no visitors, cards or flowers. In fact, I have never seen a card or flowers in anybody's hospital room in all the times I have been in the hospital.

You will also note, that coming out of the hospital is often more challenging than going in because the routine that you have been forced to follow is suddenly gone and you are left to your own devices. Many people fail at this time, and often have to be readmitted. They will need all the support you can give them.

Be sure to encourage your loved one to make a crisis plan when they are well. It is easy to put this off, I have done it myself, but it is an essential part of taking good care of yourself when you have bipolar 1.

Before we go

Summing it up

By now you should be very well versed in bipolar 1 and all its challenges. Hopefully, you will have put some of my suggestions into practice and can see for yourself that a disciplined life style can really have an effect on your illness.

Sometimes, you get complacent with bipolar 1, thinking you have beaten it, especially when you have a long euthymic period. But nothing could be further from the truth. Bipolar 1 has a sneaky way of coming round the corner with yet another new episode for you to contend with. That is why it is important to get into a regular routine and do all you can to work on your illness.

It is sad that you have to pay so much attention to your health when other people are totally free of problems, but that is the way it is. There is nothing you can do to change that. So, be prepared, do your best, and I am quite certain that you will be able to beat this disorder.

If you have tried and failed along the way, don't be discouraged. As you know, when you fall off the horse, you get right back on it again. If you are determined to beat this illness, you will.

Just make sure you are taking your medication and that the doctor is giving you the best medication cocktail possible. If your medicines are not working well, go back to see him again, and don't be afraid to change them until you start to feel better.

Be sure to keep all your appointments with doctors and therapists as these professionals are very important in maintaining your health. If you cannot find a suitable doctor, I hope you have a good support system you can rely on when you need them. They say, man is not an island, and there is a lot of truth to that.

Do take responsibility yourself to do what you can to get well and stay well. I have given you many guidelines, and I hope you will follow them. At the back of this book, you will find a **THINGS TO DO EVERY DAY** page which will help you cope with the disorder on a daily basis. Don't forget to use this guide as it will help you get through tough times. If you want to customize it for your own use, then by all means do so.

This is where we must part company. It has been a pleasure writing this book for you. I hope you have enjoyed reading it and will find it useful on your journey to wellness.

If you need any further assistance, please contact me on my website.

I have great faith in you and your efforts. I want to see you well and happy. And I know you can do it if you try.

Good luck.

Sally Alter

Family and friends

First of all, thank you for reading this book. It means the world to me that you want to help your loved one get well. They are very lucky indeed that you have shown an interest in helping them. It is not everybody who is so lucky.

I do hope you have learned a lot about this disorder and can use this information to support your loved one as best you can. The information included in this book should empower you to feel confident in understanding the problems someone with bipolar 1 faces every day.

You can encourage them to check on their **THINGS TO DO EVERY DAY** page (overleaf) and use their Daily Wellness Plan binder in order to stay on top of this illness.

Most of all, I have to emphasize that the way to cope with this situation is to take good care of yourself first. It is no use you trying to help them if you are worn out and depressed yourself. You know what they say, put on your own oxygen mask before your child's if the plane is about to crash. That applies to this plan as well.

So, thank you once again. And be well.

Sally Alter

Things to do every day

I realize it is very difficult to live your life peacefully knowing that another bipolar 1 episode may well be waiting for you when you let your guard down. That's why, when you live with such a serious illness, it is imperative that you manage it daily.

If you do even half of this plan, I am quite sure you will notice the difference in your mood swings. People who don't plan ahead get caught unawares. Don't let that be you.

The list that follows is my daily plan to get well and stay well with bipolar 1 disorder. Here is the plan I follow, even today:

- Go to bed and get up at the same time every day
- Stick to your morning routine
- Take your medication
- Eat a nutritious diet
- Eat at regular meal times
- Write in your Gratitude journal
- Journal

- Check in with how you are feeling today
  - Physically
  - Mentally
  - Emotionally
- Connect with others
- Sit in the sun for 15 minutes every day
- Drink plenty of water
- Relax and do meditation
- Do something creative
- Exercise
- Do something for fun

We have covered many of these topics, so you will be very familiar with them by now. I do hope you will put some of them into practice. If you want to devise your own plan, that would be fine as it will help you stick to it more frequently.

I am only too aware that it is difficult to keep to a daily plan when you have such a serious illness as bipolar 1. However, if you manage to do it, even through your various episodes, you will have a greater chance of success.

Good luck.

List of exercises

References

- Bipolar disorders, American Psychiatric Association, *www.psychiatry.org/patients-families/bipolar-disorders*

- Bipolar Disorder, NAMI (National Alliance on Mental Illness, *www.nami.org/About-Mental-Illness/Mental-Health-Conditions/Bipolar-Disorder*

- What is bipolar? *Bphope.com*

- Mood Disorders Association of BC, Bipolar Disorder: Effects on the family. *www.heretohelp.bc.ca/infosheet/bipolar-disorder-effects-on-the-family*

- Vann, Madeline R. MPH (author). Medically reviewed by Bass III, Pat F. MD. MPH. Is It Bipolar Disorder or Something Else? Everyday Health, *www.everydayhealth.com/bipolar-disorders/is-it-bipolar-disorder-or-something-else*

- Bipolar Disorder – Symptoms and Causes, Mayo Clinic, *www.mayoclinic.org/diseases-conditions/biopolar-disorder*

- Truschel, Jessica. Bipolar Definitian and DSM-5 Diagnostic Criteria, Psycom, *www.psycom.net/bipolar-definition-dsm-5/*

- Rapid Cycling, DBSA. *www.dbsalliance.org/education/bipolar-disoreder/rapid-cycling-bipolar*

- Raypole, Crystal., medically reviewed by Ditzell, Jeffrey. What is Bipolar Disorder with Mixed Features, Psych Central. March 4, 2021. *www.psychcentral.com/disorders/mixed-episode-symptoms, DSM -5)*

- Erica, Cirino, (author), White a., Marney, PhD.MS.Psych. Can You Have Bipolar Disorder and an Anxiety Disorder at the Same Time, Healthline, 12.28.20. *www healthline.com/health/bipolar-and-anxiety*

- Holland, Kimberely, author, Legg, Timothy, J. PhD. PsyD. medical reviewer, Bipolar Disorder and Anger: Why it happens and how to cope. 1/31/21. Healthline. *www. healthline.com/health/bipolar-disorder/bipolar-anger/*

- Mann, Denise, Bipolar and Anger: Understanding and getting control of irritability, 7/21/21.BPHope. *www.bphope.com/bipolar-anger-unravel-your-wrath/*

- Atkins, Charles, M.D., The Bipolar Disorder Answer Book, Sourcebooks.Inc.. 2007

- Burges, Wes, M.D., PhD., The Bipolar Handbook, Avery, a member of Penguin Group (USA) Inc., 2006

- Paquette, Andrea., How to Cope when Managing Bipolar becomes Overwhelming., BPhope. 8/15/19. *www.bphope.com/blog/strategies-for-bipolar-disorder-when-it-all-becomes-overwhelming/*

- Tyler, Lizzy. M.D. TalkBipolarDisorder, You Tube. 5/10/20

- Treating Mental Health in Menopausal Women. HCPLive. YouTube. 1/18/19

- Bipolar Disorder., NAMI, *https://www.nami.org/About-Mental-Illness/Mental-Health-Conditions/Bipolar-Disorder*

- Drugs to Treat Bipolar Disorder, Healthline Editorial Team, Carter, Alan, Pharm.D., 11/6/19. *www.healthline.com/health/bipolar-disorder#treatment*

- Marks, Tracy, M.D., Three Signs Your Mania is Coming (The Manic Prodrome), YouTube, 2/6/19

- Pagan, Camille, Noe. Author., Swiner, Carmelita, M.D., Does Cognitive Behavioral Therapy Treat Depression, 10122/20. *www.webmd.com/depression/guide/cognitive-behavioral-therapy-for-depression*

- Cognitive Behavioral Therapy, Mayo Clinic. *www.mayoclinic.org/tests-procedures/cognitive-behavioral-therapy/about/pac-20384610*

- Bhandari, Smitha. M.D. Antipsychotic Medication for Bipolar Disorder 4/14/20. WebMD *www.webmd.com/bipolar-disorder/guide/antipsychotic-medication*

- Atkins, Charles. M.D., The Bipolar Disorder Answer Book, Sourcebooks, Inc. 2007.

- Nall, Rachel, MSN, CRNA, Healthline 4/23/19. *www.healthline.com/health/bipolar-disorder/antidepressants*

- Hall-Flavin, Daniel K. MD. Mayo Clinic. *www.mayoclinic.org/diseases-conditions/bipolar-disorder/expert-answers/bipolar-treatment/faq-20058042*

- Ponte, Katherine, B.A., J.D., MBA, CPRP, Bipolar Depression the Lows we Don't Talk About. 9/22/21.NAMI. *www.nami.org/Blogs/NAMI-Blog/September-2021/Bipolar-Depression-The-Lows-We-Don-t-Talk-About-Enough*

- Bhandari, Smitha., MD. Bipolar Disorder and Suicide. 7/20/20. WebMD. *www.webmd.com/bipolar-disorder/guide/bipolar-disorder-suicide*

- Bipolar Disorder, Mayo Clinic. *www.mayoclinic.org/diseases-conditions/bipolar-disorder/diagnosis-treatment/drc-20355961*

- Bhandari, Smitha., MD. Psychotherapy for Bipolar Disorder. 9/23/20. WebMD. *www.webmd.com/bipolar-disorder/guide/psychotherapy-bipolar-disorder*

- Therapy. DBSA (Depression and Bipolar Support Alliance). *www.dbsalliance.org/wellness/treatment-options/therapy/*

- Vann, Madeline, R. MPH, The Link Between Bipolar Disorder and Sleep.3/26/14. Medically reviewed by Sohrabi, Farrokh, MD. Everyday Health, *https://www.everydayhealth.com/hs/bipolar-depression/bipolar-disorder-and-sleep/*

- Marks, Tracey, MD., Here's a Diet That Treats Depression (Bipolar 1), 9/25/19. YouTube.

- Vann, Madeleine, R., MPH Medically reviewed by Young, Alison, MD. 5 Foods to Avoid if You Have Bipolar Disorder. 1/18/21. Everyday Health, *www.everydayhealth.com/bipolar-disorder/the-five-worst-foods-for-bipolar-disorder.aspx*

- Krans, Brian. Medically reviewed by Legg, Timothy, J. PhD, PsyD. Foods and Nutrients for Mania and Depression. 7/6/20. *www.healthline.com/health/bipolar-disorder/foods-for-mania-and-depression*

- Staying Healthy, The Health Benefits of Tai chi.8 /20/19. Harvard Health Publishing. *www.harvard.edu/staying-healthy/the-health-benefits-of-tai-chi*

- Tai chi: A gentle way to fight stress. Stress Management , Mayo Clinic, *www.mayoclinic.org/healthy-lifestyle/stress/management/in-depth/tai-chi/art*

- Davidson, Katey, MScFN. RD, CPT. Medically reviewed by Sullivan, Courtney, Certified Yoga Instructor. Qigong Meditation Techniques: Benefits and How to Do it. Healthline. *www.healthline.com/nutrition/qigong-meditation*

- Dallas, Mary Elizabeth. Medically Reviewed by Young, Allison. 7 Triggers That Can Cause Bipolar Episodes. 1/18/21. Everyday Health. *www.everydayhealth.com/bipolar-disorder/triggers-that-cause-bipolar-episodes/*

- Tartakovsky, Margarita. MS. Currin-Sheehan, Kristen. Medically reviewed by Cassell. C.C. PsyD. Rinse, Repeat. Besting Bipolar Disorder with Routines. Psych Central. 2/18/21. *https://psychcentral.com/bipolar/building-a-routine-when-you-have-bipolar*

- Marks, Tracy. M.D., Three Signs Your Maia is Coming: The Manic Prodrome. YouTube 2/6/19.

- Cohen, Misha Ruth, 6 Qigong Exercises for Cultivating Healing Energy. Uplift. *www. uplift.love/6-qigong-exercises-for-cultivating-healing-energy/*

- Why DBT Therapy Techniques are Effective for Bipolar Treatment, GenPsych, 10/1720. *https://www.genpsych.com/post/why-dbt-therapy-techniques-are-effective-for-bipolar-disorder-treatment*

- Strong, Allison, How DBT Helps Me Deal with Bipolar Disorder, International Bipolar Foundation. *https://ibpf.org/how-dbt-helps-me-deal-with-bipolar-disorder/*

Index

Author bio

Sally Alter is a prolific writer, a sufferer of bipolar for over 50 years, and a Registered Nurse. After writing over 3000 answers on the popular site Quora—800 on bipolar alone—she realized her knowledge, compiled and condensed into books, could really help people. Sally published her first book "How to Live with Bipolar" at 73, has now published her second book, "Bipolar 1 Rescue Plan: A Practical Guide for You and Your Family" at 74, and has no plans to stop writing any time soon. Helping other people and their families and friends through the stress and struggle of bipolar has become her passion.

Sally currently resides in Texas, but she's traveled all over the US in an RV and has visited countless European countries. When she's not writing, she can be found creating stunning oil paintings, sketching with colored pencils, reading, completing jigsaw puzzles, and spending time with her beloved cat, Greta. Sally hopes that her writing will fill the gaps left behind by other bipolar disorder books to help people live more complete lives.

Sally Alter

http://sallyalter.com

Thank you for reading this book. I do hope it was helpful and you understand your illness better now.

Please consider leaving a review on Amazon.

If you need any help with your bipolar 1, please contact me on my website. We can also arrange a Zoom meeting if you prefer. I would love to hear from you.

All the very best to you,
Sally Alter
http://sallyalter.com

Author of:

• How to Live with Bipolar

• Bipolar 1 Rescue Plan: A Practical Guide for You and Your Family

The National Suicide Prevention Hotline:
1 800-273-8255